CW00391405

PUDDINGS & DESSERTS

UK COOKERY EDITOR
Katie Swallow

EDITORIAL
Food Editor: Rachel Blackmore
Assistant Food Editor: Anneka Mitchell
Home Economist: Donna Hay
Recipe Development: Lucy Andrews Sheryle
Eastwood
Editorial Coordinator: Margaret Kelly
Subeditor: Ella Martin

PHOTOGRAPHY
Ashley Mackevicius

STYLING
Susie Smith, Anna Phillips,
Wendy Berecry (cover)

DESIGN AND PRODUCTION
Manager: Sheridan Carter
Layout: Lulu Dougherty
Finished Art: Stephen Joseph
Cover Design: Frank Pithers

PUBLISHER
Philippa Sandall

© J.B. Fairfax Press Pty Ltd, 1991
This book is copyright. No part may be
reproduced or transmitted by any process
without the written permission of the publishers.

Includes Index
ISBN 1 86343 078 4 (pbk)
ISBN 1 85391 242 5

Formatted by J.B. Fairfax Press Pty Ltd
Output by Adtype, Sydney
Printed by Toppan Printing Co, Hong Kong

Distributed by J.B. Fairfax Press Pty Ltd
9 Trinity Centre, Park Farm Estate
Wellingborough, Northants
Ph: (0933) 402330 Fax: (0933) 402234

Indulge yourself with chocolate, cool off with homemade ice cream, finish the perfect meal with the perfect dessert. Whether it's a family dinner, a special birthday, a festive occasion, a dessert for supper or just because you need a treat, this is the book for you. It is packed with sumptuous desserts to suit any meal.

In this book you will find special features on pastry, and the professional decorating tips and napkin folding will add the final touch to any meal. In the Masterclass, we have chosen step-by-step recipes to show how easy it is to make spectacular-looking desserts.

CONTENTS

THE PANTRY SHELF

Unless otherwise stated the following ingredients used in this book are:

Cream   Double, suitable for whipping

Flour   White flour, plain or standard

Sugar   White sugar

WHAT'S IN A TABLESPOON?

NEW ZEALAND
1 tablespoon   15 mL   3 teaspoons

UNITED KINGDOM
1 tablespoon   15 mL   3 teaspoons

AUSTRALIA
1 tablespoon   20 mL   4 teaspoons

The recipes in this book were tested in Australia where a 20 mL tablespoon is standard. All measures are level.

The tablespoon in the New Zealand and United Kingdom sets of measuring spoons is 15 mL. In many recipes this difference will not matter. For recipes using baking powder, gelatine, bicarbonate of soda, small quantities of flour and cornflour, simply add another teaspoon for each tablespoon specified.

CANNED FOOD

Can sizes vary between countries and manufacturers. You may find the quantities in this book are slightly different from what is available. Purchase and use the can size nearest to the suggested size in the recipe.

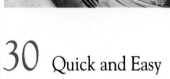

COOL DESSERTS
for hot days

C ool, refreshing desserts
make the perfect finish to a
summer's day. When you want a
traditional dessert with a difference,
try the Orange and Lime Cheesecake.
Or for a more exotic occasion,
the Coconut Soup with
Lime Sorbet

*Top: The Bishop's Hat
(see page 77)
Right: Orange and Lime
Cheesecake (recipe page 7)*

Plate, platter, cup and saucer Limoges

ORANGE AND LIME CHEESECAKE

Orange and lime team together in this delicious dessert that looks like a flan but tastes like a cheesecake.

Serves 8
Oven temperature 180°C, 350°F, Gas 4

- ☐ **155 g/5 oz plain sweet biscuits, crushed**
- ☐ **90 g/3 oz butter, melted**
- ☐ **desiccated coconut, toasted**

ORANGE AND LIME FILLING
- ☐ **185 g/6 oz cream cheese, softened**
- ☐ **2 tablespoons brown sugar**
- ☐ **1½ teaspoons finely grated orange rind**
- ☐ **1½ teaspoons finely grated lime rind**
- ☐ **3 teaspoons lime juice**
- ☐ **3 teaspoons orange juice**
- ☐ **1 egg, lightly beaten**
- ☐ **½ cup/125 mL/4 fl oz sweetened condensed milk**
- ☐ **2 tablespoons cream (double), whipped**

1 Combine biscuits and butter in a bowl and mix to combine. Press biscuit mixture over base and sides of a well-greased 23 cm/9 in flan tin with removable base. Bake for 5-8 minutes, then remove from oven and set aside to cool.

2 To make filling, place cream cheese, sugar, orange and lime rind, and orange and lime juice in a mixing bowl and beat until creamy. Beat in egg, then mix in condensed milk and fold in cream.

3 Spoon mixture into prepared case and bake for 25-30 minutes or until just firm. Turn oven off and allow cheesecake to cool in oven with door ajar. Chill before serving. Serve decorated with toasted coconut.

Orange and Lemon Cheesecake: When limes are unavailable lemon rind and juice can be used instead of the lime rind and juice to make an equally delicious cheesecake.

NECTARINE TIMBALES WITH ORANGE SAUCE

These melt-in-the-mouth desserts are just as delectable made with peeled peaches.

Serves 6

- ☐ **⅓ cup/90 mL/3 fl oz water**
- ☐ **6 nectarines, halved and stones removed**
- ☐ **½ cup/125 g/4 oz sugar**
- ☐ **⅓ cup/90 mL/3 fl oz orange juice**
- ☐ **8 teaspoons gelatine**
- ☐ **1 cup/250 mL/8 fl oz cream (double), whipped**
- ☐ **1 tablespoon Cointreau (orange liqueur)**

ORANGE SAUCE
- ☐ **1 cup/250 mL/8 fl oz orange juice**
- ☐ **rind ½ orange, cut into strips**
- ☐ **1 tablespoon sugar**
- ☐ **2 tablespoons Cointreau (orange liqueur)**
- ☐ **2 teaspoons arrowroot blended with 4 teaspoons water**

1 Place water, nectarine halves, sugar and orange juice in a saucepan. Bring just to the boil, then reduce heat and simmer for 4-5 minutes or until nectarines are soft. Using a slotted spoon remove nectarines from saucepan and set aside. Sprinkle gelatine over hot liquid in saucepan and stir to dissolve.

2 Place nectarines (including skin) and syrup in a food processor or blender and process until smooth. Push mixture through a sieve to remove any pieces of skin. Place cream in a large bowl and fold in nectarine mixture and Cointreau. Spoon mixture into six lightly oiled timbale moulds, cover and refrigerate until set.

3 To make sauce, place orange juice, orange rind, sugar, Cointreau and arrowroot mixture in a small saucepan. Cook over a medium heat until mixture boils and thickens. Remove from heat and set aside to cool. Unmould timbale and serve with sauce.

Cook's tip: If you do not have timbale moulds you can use small, attractively shaped ramekins or teacups instead for this recipe. If using ramekins, choose ones that have a 1 cup/250 mL/8 fl oz capacity.

LAYERED-FRUIT TERRINE

Layers of summer fruit set in tropical-flavoured mousse, is the ideal dessert when feeding a crowd.

Serves 10

- ☐ **1 star fruit (carambola), sliced**
- ☐ **1 peach, peeled, stoned and sliced**

MANGO LAYER
- ☐ **1 cup/250 mL/8 fl oz mango purée**
- ☐ **2 tablespoons caster sugar**
- ☐ **2 tablespoons Cointreau (orange liqueur)**
- ☐ **4 teaspoons gelatine dissolved in ⅓ cup/90 mL/3 fl oz hot water, cooled**
- ☐ **¾ cup/185 mL/6 fl oz cream (double), whipped**

PASSION FRUIT LAYER
- ☐ **½ cup/125 mL/4 fl oz passion fruit pulp**
- ☐ **2 tablespoons orange juice**
- ☐ **2 tablespoons caster sugar**
- ☐ **2 tablespoons Midori (melon liqueur)**
- ☐ **4 teaspoons gelatine dissolved in ⅓ cup/90 mL/3 fl oz hot water, cooled**
- ☐ **¾ cup/185 mL/6 oz cream (double), whipped**

1 Arrange slices of star fruit over base and sides of a lightly oiled glass or ceramic 9 x 23 cm/3½ x 9½ in loaf dish.

2 To make Mango Layer, combine mango purée, sugar and Cointreau in a large bowl. Stir in gelatine mixture and fold in cream. Pour carefully over fruit in loaf dish and refrigerate until firm.

3 To make Passion Fruit Layer, combine passion fruit pulp, orange juice, sugar and Midori in a large bowl. Stir in gelatine mixture and fold in cream.

4 Place a layer of peach slices over set Mango Layer, then carefully top with passion fruit mixture and refrigerate until set. To serve, unmould terrine and cut into slices.

Cook's tip: Run a spatula around the edge of the terrine to free it from the sides of the dish, before turning out.

Nectarine Timbales with Orange Sauce,
Layered-Fruit Terrine

7

WHITE CHOCOLATE AND RASPBERRY ICE CREAM

White chocolate and fresh raspberries are the perfect combination for this summer ice cream.

Serves 8

- ☐ 1¼ cups/315 g/10 oz sugar
- ☐ ½ cup/125 mL/4 fl oz water
- ☐ 6 egg yolks
- ☐ 1 teaspoon vanilla essence
- ☐ 250 g/8 oz white chocolate, melted
- ☐ 2 cups/500 mL/16 fl oz cream (double), whipped
- ☐ 500 g/1 lb raspberries, roughly chopped

1 Place sugar and water in a small saucepan and cook over a low heat, stirring constantly, until sugar dissolves. Bring to the boil, then reduce heat and simmer for 5 minutes or until syrup reduces by half.

2 Place egg yolks in a large mixing bowl and beat until thick and creamy. Continue beating, adding syrup in a thin stream. Add vanilla essence and chocolate and beat until mixture thickens and is cool.

3 Fold cream and raspberries into chocolate mixture. Place in a large freezerproof container, cover and freeze until firm.

Serving suggestion: Serve scoops of ice cream with fresh raspberries or berries of your choice.

DOUBLE ZABAGLIONE SOUFFLE WITH TUILES

Serves 4
Oven temperature 200°C, 400°F, Gas 6

- ☐ 6 egg yolks
- ☐ ½ cup/100 g/3½ oz caster sugar
- ☐ 1 cup/250 mL/8 fl oz cream (double), whipped
- ☐ 4 teaspoons gelatine dissolved in ¼ cup/60 mL/2 fl oz hot water, cooled
- ☐ 60 g/2 oz dark chocolate, grated
- ☐ 1½ tablespoons Tia Maria (coffee liqueur)
- ☐ 1 teaspoon instant coffee powder dissolved in 1 teaspoon hot water, cooled

GOLDEN TUILES
- ☐ ⅔ cup/170 g/5½ oz sugar
- ☐ ½ cup/60 g/2 oz flour, sifted
- ☐ 45 g/1½ oz ground almonds
- ☐ 1 egg, lightly beaten
- ☐ 2 egg whites, lightly beaten
- ☐ 75 g/2½ oz butter, melted
- ☐ 4 teaspoons water
- ☐ 75 g/2½ oz flaked almonds

1 Place egg yolks and sugar in a heatproof bowl and place over a saucepan

Double Zabaglione Soufflé with Tuiles, White Chocolate and Raspberry Ice Cream, Hazelnut Pinwheels

of simmering water and cook, beating, for 5-10 minutes or until mixture is thick and fluffy. Remove from heat and place bowl over a pan of ice and continue to beat until mixture is cool.

2   Fold cream and gelatine mixture into egg yolk mixture. Divide mixture in two and fold chocolate and Tia Maria into one portion and coffee mixture into the other.

3   Spoon each mixture, alternately, into individual soufflé dishes with 3 cm/1¹⁄₄ in high aluminium foil collars attached. Swirl by dragging a skewer through the mixture and refrigerate until set.

4   To make tuiles, place sugar, flour, ground almonds, egg, egg whites, butter and water in a bowl and mix to combine. Place teaspoonfuls of mixture on greased and lined baking trays and spread out to form a 7.5 cm/3 in circle. Sprinkle with flaked almonds and bake for 5-6 minutes or until just set around the edges. Remove from tray and shape over a rolling pin with almond side facing outwards. Allow to cool on rolling pin. Serve soufflés with tuiles.

Cook's tip: Any tuiles left over can be stored in an airtight container to serve with another dessert.

HAZELNUT PINWHEELS

An impressive-looking dessert in the style of a roulade. You will be surprised just how easy these pinwheels are to make.

Serves 10
Oven temperature 180°C, 350°F, Gas 4

- ☐ **5 eggs, separated**
- ☐ **³⁄₄ cup/170 g/5¹⁄₂ oz caster sugar**
- ☐ **125 g/4 oz hazelnuts, toasted and finely chopped**
- ☐ **¹⁄₄ cup/30 g/1 oz self-raising flour, sifted**

CHOCOLATE HAZELNUT FILLING
- ☐ **¹⁄₂ cup/125 mL/4 fl oz cream (double), whipped**
- ☐ **155 g/5 oz chocolate hazelnut spread**

1   Place egg yolks and sugar in a mixing bowl and beat until thick and creamy. Fold in hazelnuts and flour.

2   Beat egg whites until soft peaks form and fold into hazelnut mixture in two separate additions. Pour into a greased and lined 26 x 32 cm/10¹⁄₂ x 12³⁄₄ in Swiss roll tin and bake for 20-25 minutes or until cooked. Place a clean damp teatowel over roll and set aside to cool in tin.

3   Turn cold roll onto a piece of greaseproof paper sprinkled with caster sugar. Spread with hazelnut spread and cream, and roll up from short end. Chill until required.

Serving suggestion: Cut into slices, serve with extra cream and decorate with chopped hazelnuts.

Freeze it: This roll is also delicious filled with just the chocolate hazelnut spread. This variation freezes well and will slice evenly if cut while still frozen and allowed to thaw in serving dishes for 20 minutes.

Ice cream bowl/ Peter Crisp, The Australian Craftworks *Blue plate* Cydoma, The Glass Studio

This wonderful dessert fulfils every chocoholic's dream. It takes a little time to prepare, but is well worth the effort.

TRIPLE-CHOCOLATE TERRINE

Serves 10
Oven temperature 180°C, 350°F, Gas 4

BUTTER CAKE
☐ **125 g/4 oz butter**
☐ **1 teaspoon vanilla essence**
☐ **1/2 cup/100 g/31/2 oz caster sugar**
☐ **2 eggs**
☐ **1 cup/125 g/4 oz self-raising flour, sifted**
☐ **1/3 cup/90 mL/3 fl oz milk**

DARK CHOCOLATE FUDGE FILLING
☐ **125 g/4 oz butter**
☐ **2 tablespoons icing sugar**
☐ **90 g/3 oz dark chocolate, melted and cooled**
☐ **1 cup/250 mL/8 fl oz cream (double), chilled**

MILK CHOCOLATE MOUSSE
☐ **200 g/61/2 oz milk chocolate, chopped**
☐ **125 g/4 oz unsalted butter**
☐ **2 eggs**
☐ **2 tablespoons caster sugar**
☐ **1 cup/250 mL/8 fl oz cream (double)**
☐ **1 tablespoon dark rum**
☐ **6 teaspoons gelatine dissolved in 2 tablespoons hot water, cooled**

WHITE CHOCOLATE GLAZE
☐ **250 g/8 oz white chocolate**
☐ **100 g/31/2 oz unsalted butter**

1   To make cake, place butter and vanilla essence in a mixing bowl and beat until light and fluffy. Gradually add sugar, beating well after each addition, until mixture is creamy. Beat in eggs one at a time. Fold flour and milk, alternately, into butter mixture. Spoon mixture into a greased and lined 11 x 21 cm/41/2 x 81/2 in loaf tin and bake for 20-25 minutes or until cooked when tested with a skewer. Stand in tin for 5 minutes, then turn onto a wire rack to cool.

2   To make fudge filling, beat butter and icing sugar until creamy. Fold in chocolate,
then cream. Refrigerate until required.

3   To make mousse, place chocolate and butter in a saucepan and cook over a low heat, stirring constantly, until well blended. Remove from heat and set aside to cool. Place eggs and sugar in a bowl and beat until thick and creamy. Fold in chocolate mixture, cream, rum and gelatine mixture.

4   To assemble terrine, cut cake horizontally into three layers. Spread 2 layers with fudge filling and place one of these layers, filling side upwards, in the base of an 11 x 21 cm/41/2 x 81/2 in loaf tin

lined with plastic food wrap. Top with half the chocolate mousse and refrigerate for 10 minutes or until almost set. Place the second layer of filling-topped cake over the mousse with filling facing upwards. Top with remaining mousse and refrigerate until almost set. Place remaining cake layer on top and refrigerate until set.

5   To make glaze, place chocolate and butter in a small saucepan and cook over a low heat, stirring constantly, until well blended. Set aside and cool slightly. Turn terrine onto a wire rack, trim edges, pour glaze over to cover and allow to set.

1 Spread 2 layers of cake with fudge filling and place one of these layers, filling side upwards, in the base of a loaf tin lined with plastic food wrap. Top with half the chocolate mousse and refrigerate.

2 Turn terrine onto a wire rack, pour glaze over to cover and allow to set.

Glasses, platter and plates Mosman Antique Centre

11

MANGO COCONUT SOUP WITH LIME SORBET

Serves 6

LIME SORBET
- ☐ ¹/₂ cup/125 g/4 oz sugar
- ☐ ¹/₂ cup/125 mL/4 fl oz water
- ☐ ¹/₂ cup/125 mL/4 fl oz white wine
- ☐ ¹/₂ cup/125 mL/4 fl oz lime juice
- ☐ 2 teaspoons finely grated lime rind
- ☐ 1 egg white

MANGO COCONUT SOUP
- ☐ 1.5 kg/3 lb mangoes, peeled, seeded and chopped
- ☐ ¹/₃ cup/90 mL/3 fl oz freshly squeezed orange juice
- ☐ ³/₄ cup/185 mL/6 fl oz water
- ☐ ¹/₄ cup/60 mL/ 2 fl oz green ginger wine
- ☐ 2 cups/500 mL/16 fl oz coconut milk, chilled

1   To make sorbet, place sugar, water and wine in a saucepan and cook, stirring, over a low heat until sugar dissolves. Bring to the boil, then reduce heat and simmer, uncovered, for 5 minutes. Remove from heat and set aside to cool.

2   Add lime juice and rind to sugar syrup, spoon into a freezerproof container, cover and freeze until firm. Remove sorbet from freezer, place in a clean bowl and beat until smooth. Beat egg white until stiff peaks form, then fold into lime mixture. Return mixture to freezerproof container, cover and freeze until completely solid.

3   To make soup, place mangoes in a food processor or blender and purée. Add orange juice, water and ginger wine and process until combined. Chill well.

To serve: Stir coconut milk into soup. Spoon soup into six bowls and top with scoops of sorbet.

WHITE CHOCOLATE MOUSSE WITH COULIS

Serves 8

CHOCOLATE MOUSSE
- ☐ 185 g/6 oz white chocolate
- ☐ 30 g/1 oz butter
- ☐ 4 egg yolks
- ☐ ¹/₃ cup/75 g/2¹/₂ oz caster sugar
- ☐ 2 teaspoons brandy
- ☐ 1¹/₂ cups/375 mL/12 fl oz cream (double), whipped

PEACH COULIS
- ☐ 440 g/14 oz canned peaches in natural juice, drained
- ☐ 1 tablespoon caster sugar
- ☐ 1 tablespoon Cointreau (orange liqueur) (optional)

1   To make mousse, place chocolate and butter in a small saucepan and cook over a low heat, stirring, until melted and well

Glasses Corso di Fiori Plate, bowl Sally Portnoy, The Australian Craftworks

12

blended. Remove from heat and set aside to cool.

2   Place egg yolks, sugar and brandy in a large heatproof bowl, place over a saucepan of simmering water and cook, beating, until thick and fluffy. Remove bowl from heat and continue to beat until mixture is cool. Mix in chocolate mixture and fold in cream. Spoon into serving glasses and refrigerate until firm.

3   To make coulis, place peaches, sugar and Cointreau, if using, in a food processor or blender and process until smooth. Push coulis through a sieve.

Serving suggestion: Spoon coulis over mousse in glasses or serve separately.

Cook's tip: This mousse is also delicious served with an apricot or raspberry coulis.

SUMMER WINE JELLY

Almost any fresh fruit can be used to make this dessert. You should avoid pineapple, pawpaw and kiwifruit as they contain an enzyme which prevents the jelly from setting.

Serves 8

- ☐ **4 apricots, stoned and halved**
- ☐ **200 g/6¹/₂ oz green grapes**
- ☐ **250 g/8 oz strawberries, hulled and halved**
- ☐ **250 g/8 oz fresh or canned cherries, stoned**
- ☐ **60 g/2 oz gelatine dissolved in ¹/₂ cup/125 mL/4 fl oz hot water, cooled**
- ☐ **2 cups/500 mL/16 fl oz sweet white wine**
- ☐ **2 cups/500 mL/16 fl oz apple juice**
- ☐ **¹/₃ cup/90 mL/3 fl oz Midori (melon liqueur) or additional apple juice**

1   Place apricots, grapes, strawberries and cherries in a bowl and toss to combine.

2   Place gelatine mixture, wine, apple juice and Midori or additional apple juice in a bowl and mix to combine. Pour one-quarter of the wine mixture into a lightly oiled 4 cup/1 litre/1³/₄ pt capacity mould and top with one-quarter of the fruit. Place in refrigerator to set.

Plate Waterford Wedgwood

3   Repeat with remaining liquid and fruit. When jelly is set unmould and serve garnished with extra fruit if desired.

Unmoulding a gelatine dessert: Moulded gelatine desserts need to be loosened before you try to turn them out. This is easily done by placing the mould in warm water for a few seconds. After removing mould from water dry the base and tip it sideways, while at the same time gently pulling the mixture away from the edge of the mould. This breaks the air lock. Rinse the serving plate with cold water and place upside down on top of the mould. Then, holding firmly, quickly turn over both mould and plate and give a sharp shake. The dessert should fall onto the plate. If it refuses to move, place a hot, wet cloth over the base of the mould for 10-20 seconds. Wetting the plate means that you can easily move the dessert if it does not land in the centre when you unmould it.

Left: White Chocolate Mousse with Coulis, Mango Coconut Soup with Lime Sorbet, Above: Summer Wine Jelly

light, refreshing
COOL ICES

BASIC MOUSSE-BASED VANILLA ICE CREAM

Makes 1 litre/1¾ pt

- ☐ **6 egg yolks**
- ☐ **¾ cup/185 g/6 oz sugar**
- ☐ **1 cup/250 mL/8 fl oz water**
- ☐ **2 teaspoons vanilla essence**
- ☐ **3 cups/750 mL/1¼ pt cream (double), whipped**

1   Place egg yolks in a mixing bowl and beat until fluffy. Place sugar and water in a saucepan and cook over a low heat, stirring constantly, until sugar dissolves. Bring to the boil and cook until syrup reaches thread stage (107°C/225°F on a sweet thermometer).

2   Gradually pour syrup in a thin stream, into egg yolks, beating constantly, until mixture leaves a trail and is cool.

3   Fold in vanilla essence and cream. Pour into a freezerproof container and freeze until mixture begins to freeze around the edges. Beat mixture until even in texture. Return to the freezer and repeat beating process two more times. Freeze until solid.

Coffee Ice Cream: Replace vanilla essence with 2 tablespoons coffee powder dissolved in 2 tablespoons hot water and cooled. Continue as for basic recipe.

Raspberry Ice Cream: Fold 2 cups/ 500 mL/16 fl oz raspberry purée into mousse base with cream. Continue as for basic recipe. Replacing vanilla essence with 2 tablespoons Cointreau (orange liqueur) is a delicious variation.

Coconut Ice Cream: Replace ½ cup/ 125 mL/4 fl oz cream with ½ cup/125 mL/ 4 fl oz coconut cream and fold in ½ cup/ 45 g/1½ oz desiccated coconut with cream. Continue as for basic recipe. Replacing the vanilla essence with 2 tablespoons Malibu (coconut liqueur) makes an exotic variation.

WATERMELON SORBET

Alcohol prevents sorbet from freezing rock-hard.

Makes 1.2 litres/2 pt

- ☐ **⅔ cup/170 g/5½ oz sugar**
- ☐ **1¼ cups/310 mL/10 fl oz water**
- ☐ **2½ cups/625 mL/1¼ pt watermelon purée**
- ☐ **2 egg whites**

1   Place sugar and water in a saucepan and cook over a low heat, stirring, until sugar dissolves. Bring to the boil, reduce heat and simmer for 10 minutes. Remove from heat and set aside to cool.

2   Mix watermelon purée into sugar syrup, pour into a freezerproof container and freeze until almost solid.

3   Place in a food processor or blender and process until smooth. Beat egg whites until soft peaks form and fold into fruit mixture. Return to freezerproof container and freeze until solid.

Mango and Passion Fruit Sorbet: Replace watermelon purée with 2 cups/ 500 mL/16 fl oz of mango purée and the pulp of 4 passion fruit. Continue as for Watermelon Sorbet.

Kiwifruit Sorbet: Replace watermelon purée with 2 cups/500 mL/16 fl oz of kiwifruit purée, ¼ cup/60 mL/2 fl oz freshly squeezed grapefruit juice and 2 tablespoons crème de menthe (mint liqueur). Continue as for Watermelon Sorbet.

Serving suggestions: Chill the serving dishes to prevent the sorbet from melting too fast. Sorbets that do not contain alcohol should be softened in the refrigerator for 20-30 minutes before serving to make scooping easier.

BASIC CUSTARD-BASED VANILLA ICE CREAM

Makes 1.5 litres/2½ pt

- ☐ **8 egg yolks**
- ☐ **1¼ cups/280 g/9 oz caster sugar**
- ☐ **4 cups/1 L/1¾ pt milk**
- ☐ **2 cups/500 mL/16 fl oz cream (single)**
- ☐ **2 teaspoons vanilla essence**

1   Place egg yolks and sugar in a mixing bowl and beat until thick and creamy.

2   Place milk and cream in a large saucepan and bring just to the boil. Remove from heat and whisk gradually into egg yolk mixture. Return to saucepan and cook over a low heat, stirring constantly, until mixture coats the back of a wooden spoon. Remove from heat, place over a pan of ice and allow to cool to room temperature.

3   Stir in vanilla essence. Transfer to an ice cream maker and freeze according to manufacturer's instructions.

Chocolate Ice Cream: Reduce caster sugar to ¾ cup/170 g/5½ oz and fold 315 g/10 oz cooled, melted dark or milk chocolate into cooled custard. Continue as for basic recipe.

Peach Ice Cream: Purée 2 x 440 g/14 oz drained canned peaches and fold into cooled custard. Continue as for basic recipe.

Mousse-Based Ice Cream, Coffee, Raspberry and Coconut variations in Tuile Basket, Watermelon Sorbet, Mango and Passion Fruit Sorbet, Kiwifruit Sorbet, Basic Custard-Based Vanilla Ice Cream with Chocolate and Peach variations in Tuile Basket

TUILE BASKETS

Makes 6
Oven temperature 200°C, 400°F, Gas 6

- [ ] **2 egg whites**
- [ ] **1 egg**
- [ ] **1 teaspoon vanilla essence**
- [ ] **30 g/1 oz flour**
- [ ] **$\frac{1}{3}$ cup/90 g/3 oz sugar**
- [ ] **45 g/1$\frac{1}{2}$ oz unsalted butter, melted**

1 Place egg whites, egg and vanilla essence in a bowl and beat until combined. Mix in flour and sugar. Pour butter over mixture and stir in.

2 Grease the base of an upturned 20 cm/8 in round cake tin. Place a spoonful of mixture in centre of base of cake tin and spread out evenly to cover base leaving a 1 cm border. Bake for 8-10 minutes or until golden around edges. Remove tuile from base of cake tin, using a spatula, place over an inverted 8 cm/3$\frac{1}{2}$ in based ramekin and shape to form a basket. Allow tuile to cool before removing. Repeat with remaining mixture.

Cook's tip: It is best to cook only one or two tuiles at a time as they harden very quickly once removed from the oven.

Plates Cydonia, The Glass Studio

PIES AND PASTRIES

Whether it's a picnic in the park, a family dinner or a special occasion, you are sure to find the perfect pie for the occasion in this chapter. Using the hints on pastry making and the special feature on decorating pies, your pies will rival those of the professionals in next to no time.

Top: The Bishop's Hat (see page 77)
Right: Sour Cream Apple Pie
(recipe page 18)

SOUR CREAM APPLE PIE

Serves 8
Oven temperature 200°C, 400°F, Gas 6

- ☐ **315 g/10 oz prepared sweet shortcrust pastry**
- ☐ **2 tablespoons apricot jam**

APPLE FILLING
- ☐ **75 g/2¹/₂ oz butter**
- ☐ **3 Granny Smith apples, cored, peeled and sliced**
- ☐ **2 tablespoons brown sugar**

CARAMEL SAUCE
- ☐ **¹/₄ cup/60 g/2 oz sugar**
- ☐ **4 teaspoons water**
- ☐ **¹/₄ cup/60 mL/2 fl oz cream (double)**
- ☐ **30 g/1 oz butter, cut into small pieces**

SOUR CREAM TOPPING
- ☐ **500 g/1 lb sour cream**
- ☐ **4 teaspoons caster sugar**
- ☐ **1 teaspoon vanilla essence**

1   Roll pastry out and line a greased, deep 18 cm/7 in fluted flan tin with a removable base. Prick pastry base with a fork. Line pastry case with nonstick baking paper, weigh down with uncooked rice and cook for 10 minutes. Remove rice and paper and bake for 8-10 minutes longer or until pastry is golden. Place jam in a small saucepan and bring to the boil. As soon as the pastry case is cooked, brush with boiling jam and return to the oven for 3-4 minutes longer. Set pastry case aside to cool completely.

2   To make filling, melt half the butter in a large frying pan and add half the apple slices, sprinkle with half the sugar and cook, turning slices until they are tender. Remove apple slices to a plate and repeat with remaining butter, apple slices and sugar. Layer apple slices evenly in pastry case.

3   To make sauce, place sugar and water in a heavy-based saucepan and cook over a low heat, stirring until sugar dissolves. Bring to the boil and boil without stirring for 8 minutes or until mixture is a caramel colour. Occasionally brush down sides of pan with a pastry brush dipped in cold water. Reduce heat, stir in cream and continue stirring until sauce is smooth. Mix in butter and set aside to cool slightly. Using a large spoon drizzle caramel over apples in pastry case.

4   To make topping, place sour cream,

sugar and vanilla essence in a bowl and mix to combine. Spoon sour cream mixture over apples, then spread out carefully using the back of a spoon, taking mixture just to rim of pie. Reduce oven temperature to 180°C/350°F/Gas 4 and bake pie for 5-7 minutes. Allow to cool at room temperature, then refrigerate for several hours or overnight before serving.

RASPBERRY MOUSSE FLAN

A light and creamy raspberry mousse with a crisp almond pastry.

Serves 8
Oven temperature 200°C, 400°F, Gas 6

ALMOND PASTRY
- ☐ **1¹/₄ cups/155 g/5 oz flour**
- ☐ **2 tablespoons caster sugar**
- ☐ **15 g/¹/₂ oz ground almonds**
- ☐ **125 g/4 oz butter, cut into pieces**
- ☐ **1 egg yolk, lightly beaten**
- ☐ **2-3 tablespoons water, chilled**

RASPBERRY MOUSSE FILLING
- ☐ **90 g/3 oz raspberries**
- ☐ **2 eggs, separated**
- ☐ **¹/₄ cup/60 g/2 oz caster sugar**
- ☐ **¹/₂ cup/125 mL/4 fl oz cream (double), whipped**
- ☐ **8 teaspoons gelatine dissolved in ¹/₂ cup/125 mL/4 fl oz hot water, cooled to room temperature**
- ☐ **500 g/1 lb mixed berries of your choice**

1   To make pastry, place flour, sugar and almonds in a food processor and process to combine. Add butter and process until mixture resembles fine bread crumbs. With machine running add egg yolk and enough water to form a soft dough. Turn pastry onto a floured surface and knead lightly until smooth. Wrap in plastic food wrap and refrigerate for 30 minutes.

2   Roll out pastry on a lightly floured surface and line a lightly greased, deep 20 cm/8 in fluted flan tin with a removable base. Refrigerate for 15 minutes. Line pastry case with nonstick baking paper, weigh down with uncooked rice and bake for 10 minutes. Remove rice and paper and cook for 10 minutes longer or until pastry case is lightly browned and cooked.

3   To make filling, place raspberries in a food processor or blender and purée. Push

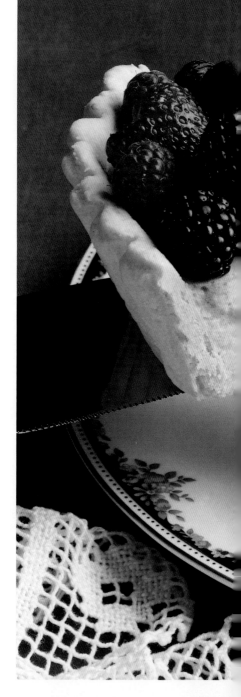

purée through a sieve, to remove seeds. Place egg yolks and sugar in a bowl and beat until thick and creamy. Place egg whites in a separate bowl and beat until stiff peaks form.

4   Fold whipped cream and egg whites into the egg yolk mixture. Then fold 4 tablespoons of egg mixture into raspberry purée. Fold half the gelatine mixture into the raspberry mixture and the remainder into the egg mixture.

5   Place large spoonfuls of egg mixture

into pastry case, then top with small spoonfuls of raspberry mixture. Repeat until both mixtures are used and pastry case is two-thirds full. Run a spatula through the mousse to swirl the mixtures. Refrigerate for 2 hours or until mousse is firm. Just prior to serving, top the flan with mixed berries.

Raspberry Mousse Flan

perfect PASTRY

❧ When making pastry have all the utensils and ingredients as cold as possible. In hot weather chill the utensils before using. Wash your hands in cold water and use only your fingertips for kneading.

❧ Always add water or liquid cautiously as the amount required can vary depending on the flour that you use.

❧ A food processor is great for making pastry as the ingredients can be mixed together in seconds. When a recipe says to rub the fat in using fingertips, you can do this in the food processor using the metal blade, then add water to form a dough.

❧ When filling pies, fill the dish or pastry case to the rim. If the pie is to be covered, pile the filling up in the centre to help support the lid. If you do not have enough filling for the pie, place an up-turned egg cup or pie funnel in the middle of the dish for support.

❧ Allow a cooked filling to cool before putting it into the pie or the pastry will be tough and soggy.

❧ Always preheat the oven before baking pastry. If pastry is put into a cold oven the fat will run and the pastry will be tough, greasy and have a poor texture.

❧ Uncooked pastry can be stored in an airtight container or sealed plastic food bag in the refrigerator for up to 3 days, or frozen for up to 3 months. Before freezing pastry, roll and shape it.

Sugar-crusted fruit baskets are ideal for entertaining as each part can be made ahead of time. Leave the final assembly until just before serving or the fruit will cause the pastry baskets to go soggy and collapse.

SUGAR-CRUSTED FRUIT BASKETS

Serves 6
Oven temperature 200°C, 400°F, Gas 6

SUGAR-CRUSTED BASKETS
- [ ] **6 sheets filo pastry**
- [ ] **60 g/3 oz butter, melted**
- [ ] **¹/₂ cup/125 g/4 oz sugar**

POACHED FRUIT
- [ ] **1 cup/250 g/8 oz sugar**
- [ ] **1 cup/250 mL/8 fl oz water**
- [ ] **¹/₂ cup/125 mL/4 fl oz white wine**
- [ ] **4 apricots, stoned and quartered**
- [ ] **4 peaches, stoned and cut into eighths**
- [ ] **4 plums, stoned and quartered**
- [ ] **4 nectarines, stoned and cut into eighths**
- [ ] **16 strawberries**

RASPBERRY CREAM
- [ ] **125 g/4 oz raspberries, puréed**
- [ ] **³/₄ cup/185 mL/6 fl oz cream (double)**
- [ ] **4 teaspoons icing sugar**

1　To make baskets, cut each pastry sheet crosswise into 8 cm/3¹/₂ in wide strips. Grease outsides of four small, round-based ramekins and place upside down on a greased baking tray. Brush pastry strips with butter and lay over ramekins, overlapping each strip, and bringing ends down to lay flat on tray. Brush again with butter and sprinkle generously with sugar. Cook for 10-15 minutes or until basket is crisp and golden.

2　To poach fruits, place sugar, water and wine in a saucepan and cook over a low heat, stirring, until sugar dissolves. Add apricots, peaches, plums and nectarines to syrup and simmer for 3-4 minutes or until fruit is just soft. Remove saucepan from heat, stir in strawberries and set aside to stand for 5 minutes. Drain.

3　To make cream, push raspberry pureé through a sieve to remove seeds. Place cream in a bowl, fold in icing sugar and purée.

To serve: Just prior to serving, place baskets on individual serving plates, fill with fruits and top with Raspberry Cream.

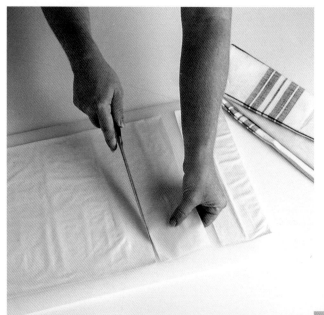

1　Cut each pastry sheet crosswise into 8 cm/3¹/₂ in wide strips. Keep the pastry sheets that you are not using covered with a damp teatowel. This stops the filo pastry from drying out and cracking.

2　Brush pastry strips with butter and lay over greased ramekins, overlapping each strip and bringing ends down to lay flat on baking tray.

Plate Waterford Wedgwood

CREAMY CARAMEL BANANA PIE

The combination of flavours in this sweet caramel pie is out of this world. It must be served well chilled so, if possible, make it the day before you wish to serve it.

Serves 8
Oven temperature 190°C, 375°F, Gas 5

- ☐ **200 g/6¹/₂ oz gingernut biscuits, crushed**
- ☐ **75 g/2¹/₂ oz butter, melted**

BANANA CARAMEL FILLING
- ☐ **1 cup/250 mL/8 fl oz sweetened condensed milk**
- ☐ **3 just-ripe bananas, sliced**

CREAM TOPPING
- ☐ **1 cup/250 mL/8 fl oz cream (double)**
- ☐ **4 teaspoons icing sugar**
- ☐ **¹/₂ teaspoon vanilla essence**

1 Place crushed biscuits and butter in a bowl and mix well to combine. Press biscuit mixture into a greased 20 cm/8 in pie plate and bake for 10 minutes. Set aside to cool completely.

2 To make filling, pour condensed milk into a shallow 20 cm/8 in pie plate. Cover completely with aluminium foil, taking the foil over the rim of the pie plate to make it airtight. Place pie plate in a baking dish with enough water to come halfway up the sides of the pie plate. Increase oven temperature to 220°C/425°F/Gas 7 and cook for 1¹/₄-1¹/₂ hours or until condensed milk is a rich caramel colour. Add more water to dish as required during cooking. Remove pie plate from baking dish and set aside to cool completely.

3 Place bananas in biscuit crust and pour caramel over to completely cover bananas.

4 To make topping, place cream, icing sugar and vanilla essence in a bowl and beat until soft peaks form. Place cream mixture in a piping bag fitted with a large fluted nozzle and pipe rosettes of cream around outside of the pie and refrigerate for at least 4 hours. This pie should be served very cold.

Serving suggestion: Serve with vanilla ice cream and sprinkling of chocolate.

Cook's tip: It can be difficult to get a clean slice from a pie made with a crumb crust. However, there is a way to ensure that your crust never sticks to the pie plate and that you will always get that perfect slice. It takes a little extra time but is worth the effort. Cut a square of aluminium foil 10 cm/4 in larger than the diameter of the pie plate. Turn the plate upside down and press foil firmly over it. Remove foil, turn pie plate right way up and press moulded foil firmly into plate. Fold the edges of the foil over the rim of the plate. Next, press crumble mixture firmly into foil-lined plate and bake as directed in recipe. Cool crust to room temperature then freeze for 1 hour or overnight – the crust must be frozen solid. Using the edges of the foil, carefully lift the crust from the plate and gently peel away the foil a little at a time. Then, supporting the base with a spatula, carefully return the crust to the pie plate.

Marble stand Corso di Fiori Blue plate and patterned plate Limoges

Creamy Caramel Banana Pie, Orange Chocolate Tart

ORANGE CHOCOLATE TARTS

Orange and chocolate are long-time favourites and no more so than in these wonderful tarts.

Serves 6
Oven temperature 200°C, 400°F, Gas 6

- ☐ **375 g/12 oz prepared shortcrust pastry**
- ☐ **125 g/4 oz dark chocolate, melted**

ORANGE FILLING
- ☐ **3 egg yolks**
- ☐ **2 tablespoons sugar**
- ☐ **1¼ cups/315 mL/10 fl oz milk, scalded**
- ☐ **1 tablespoon finely grated orange rind**
- ☐ **2 tablespoons Grand Marnier (orange liqueur)**
- ☐ **1½ teaspoons gelatine dissolved in 4 teaspoons hot water, cooled**
- ☐ **¼ cup/60 mL/2 fl oz cream (double), whipped**

1 Roll pastry out and line six 10 cm/4 in flan tins. Line pastry cases with nonstick baking paper and weigh down with uncooked rice. Bake for 8 minutes, then remove rice and paper and bake for 10 minutes longer or until pastry is golden. Set aside to cool completely. Brush cooled pastry cases with melted chocolate and set aside until chocolate sets.

2 To make filling, place egg yolks and sugar in a heatproof bowl over a saucepan of simmering water, beating until a ribbon trail forms when beater is lifted from mixture. Remove bowl from heat and gradually whisk in milk. Transfer mixture to a heavy-based saucepan and cook over a low heat, stirring in a figure eight pattern, until mixture thickens and coats the back of a wooden spoon. Do not allow the mixture to boil. Remove from heat, place in a pan of ice and stir until cool.

3 Stir in orange rind, Grand Marnier and gelatine mixture. Fold in cream, then spoon filling into pastry cases. Refrigerate until set.

Serving suggestion: Decorate tarts with quartered orange slices and fine strips of orange rind.

RHUBARB AND APPLE TART

Rhubarb and apple combine to give a new twist to a traditional recipe.

Serves 10
Oven temperature 200°C, 400°F, Gas 6

PASTRY
- ☐ 1 cup/125 g/4 oz flour, sifted
- ☐ 2 teaspoons icing sugar, sifted
- ☐ 90 g/3 oz butter, cubed
- ☐ 4 teaspoons iced water

RHUBARB AND APPLE FILLING
- ☐ 6 stalks rhubarb, chopped
- ☐ 2 tablespoons sugar
- ☐ 3 green apples, cored, peeled and sliced
- ☐ 30 g/1 oz butter
- ☐ 125 g/4 oz cream cheese
- ☐ 1/3 cup/90 g/3 oz sugar
- ☐ 1 teaspoon vanilla essence
- ☐ 1 egg

1 To make pastry, place flour and icing sugar in a bowl and rub in butter, using your fingertips, until mixture resembles coarse bread crumbs. Add water and knead to a smooth dough. Wrap in plastic food wrap and refrigerate for 30 minutes.

2 Roll out pastry on a lightly floured surface and line a greased 23 cm/9 in fluted flan tin with removable base. Line pastry case with nonstick baking paper and weigh down with uncooked rice. Bake for 15 minutes. Remove rice and paper and cook for 5 minutes longer.

3 To make filling, poach or microwave rhubarb until tender. Drain well, stir in sugar and set aside to cool. Melt butter in a frying pan and cook apples for 3-4 minutes. Remove apples from pan and set aside to cool.

4 Place cream cheese, sugar, vanilla essence and egg in a bowl and beat until smooth. Spoon rhubarb into pastry case, then top with cream cheese mixture and arrange apple slices attractively on the top. Reduce oven temperature to 180°C/350°F/Gas 4 and cook for 40-45 minutes or until filling is firm.

Cook's tip: The pastry for this tart can be made in the food processor if you wish. Place flour, icing sugar and butter in a food processor and process until mixture resembles coarse bread crumbs. With machine running add water and continue to process until a smooth dough forms.

COFFEE NUT PIE

This version of the traditional American Mud Pie is sure to be popular as a dessert or as a special afternoon tea treat.

Serves 6
- ☐ 220 g/7 oz plain chocolate biscuits, crushed
- ☐ 125 g/4 oz butter

COFFEE FILLING
- ☐ 1 litre/1¾ pt vanilla ice cream, softened
- ☐ 2 teaspoons instant coffee dissolved in 4 teaspoons hot water and cooled

CHOC-NUT TOPPING
- ☐ ½ cup/125 mL/4 fl oz evaporated milk
- ☐ ½ cup/100 g/3½ oz caster sugar
- ☐ 200 g/6½ oz dark chocolate
- ☐ 60 g/2 oz chopped pecans or walnuts

1 Place crushed biscuits and butter in a bowl and mix well to combine. Press biscuit mixture into a shallow 23 cm/9 in dish.

2 To make filling, place ice cream and coffee mixture in a bowl and mix to combine. Spoon over biscuit base and place in freezer.

3 To make topping, place evaporated milk, sugar and chocolate in a saucepan and cook, stirring, over a low heat until chocolate is melted and mixture is smooth. Stir in pecans, allow to cool, then pour topping over filling and freeze until firm.

Decorating suggestion: Top with chocolate caraques (see page 28) and whipped cream.

Rhubarb and Apple Tart, Coffee Nut Pie

Apple and Rhubarb Tart platter Villeroy and Boch

decorative touches for
FRUIT PIES

SWEET SHORTCRUST PASTRY

Homemade shortcrust pastry is easy to make if you have a food processor. This recipe is suitable to use whenever sweet shortcrust pastry is called for.

- ☐ 1½ cups/185 g/6 oz flour
- ☐ ¼ cup/30 g/1 oz cornflour
- ☐ 125 g/4 oz butter, cut into cubes
- ☐ ⅓ cup/75 g/2½ oz caster sugar
- ☐ 1 egg, lightly beaten
- ☐ 1 egg yolk, lightly beaten
- ☐ 1 teaspoon vanilla essence

1 Place flour, cornflour, butter and sugar in a food processor or blender and process until mixture resembles coarse bread crumbs. Combine egg, egg yolk and vanilla essence and with machine running add to flour mixture, continuing to process until a soft dough forms.

2 Turn dough onto a floured surface and knead lightly. Wrap in plastic food wrap and refrigerate for 30 minutes. Use as desired.

APRICOT PIE

Serves 6
Oven temperature 200°C, 400°F, Gas 6

- [ ] ¹/₂ **quantity Sweet Shortcrust Pastry (see recipe)**

APRICOT FILLING
- [ ] **3 x 440 g/14 oz canned apricot halves, drained and sliced**
- [ ] **¹/₄ cup/45 g/1¹/₂ oz brown sugar**
- [ ] **¹/₂ teaspoon ground nutmeg**
- [ ] **¹/₂ teaspoon ground cinnamon**

1 To make filling, place apricots, sugar, nutmeg and cinnamon in a bowl and mix to combine.

2 Spoon filling into a greased 23 cm/9 in pie plate. Roll out pastry to 3 mm/¹/₈ in thick. Mark centre of pastry and cut four 10 cm/4 in slits, crossing at the centre. Place pastry over filling and trim edges 5mm/¹/₄ in wider than rim of plate. Fold

back flaps of pastry from centre of pie. Make a large scalloped edge by placing your thumb against the inside pastry edge and moulding the pastry around it with fingers of other hand.

3 Bake pie for 20-30 minutes or until pastry is golden and cooked through.

APPLE PIE

Serves 6
Oven temperature 220°C, 425°F, Gas 7

- [ ] **1¹/₂ quantities Sweet Shortcrust Pastry (see recipe)**

APPLE FILLING
- [ ] **2 x 440 g/14 oz canned sliced apples**
- [ ] **¹/₄ cup/60 g/2 oz sugar**
- [ ] **¹/₂ teaspoon ground cloves**
- [ ] **¹/₂ teaspoon ground cardamom**

1 To make filling, place apples, sugar, cloves and cardamom in a bowl and mix to combine.

2 Roll out two-thirds of the pastry to 3 mm/¹/₈ in thick and line a greased 23 cm/9 in pie dish. Spoon filling into pastry shell.

3 Roll out remaining pastry and cut out apple shapes as shown in picture. Brush pastry with a little water and place apple shapes between cut-outs. Place pastry over filling, trim edge and fold under bottom pastry layer. To form rope edge, pinch edge at a slant using your thumb and index finger and at the same time pulling back with your thumb.

4 Bake pie for 20 minutes, then reduce temperature to 160°C/325°F/Gas 3 and cook for 30-40 minutes longer or until pastry is golden and cooked through.

CHERRY PIE

Serves 6
Oven temperature 220°C, 425°F, Gas 7

- [ ] **1 quantity Sweet Shortcrust Pastry (see recipe)**

CHERRY FILLING
- [ ] **3 x 440 g/14 oz canned pitted black cherries**
- [ ] **2 tablespoons brown sugar**
- [ ] **4 teaspoons flour**
- [ ] **1 teaspoon ground mixed spice**

1 To make filling, drain cherries on sheets of absorbent kitchen paper. Place cherries, sugar, flour and mixed spice in a bowl and mix to combine.

2 Roll out two-thirds of the pastry to 3 mm/¹/₈ in thick and line a greased 23 cm/9 in pie dish. Spoon filling into pastry case. Roll out remaining pastry and, using a pastry cutter, cut into 2 cm/³/₄ in wide strips. Twist each strip and arrange in a lattice pattern over filling. Brush edge of pie with a little water and seal each strip to edge.

3 Bake pie for 20 minutes, then reduce temperature to 160°C/325°F/Gas 3 and cook for 30-40 minutes longer or until pastry is golden and cooked through.

Cherry Pie, Apricot Pie, Apple Pie

Pie dishes Waterford Wedgwood

decorative touches for DESSERTS

FROSTED FRUITS

Frosted, strawberries, cherries, small bunches of grapes or redcurrants make wonderful decorations for cold desserts and cakes.

To frost fruit: Rinse fruit and drain well on absorbent kitchen paper. Break into small bunches or single pieces and remove any leaves or unwanted stems. Place an egg white in a small bowl and whisk lightly. Dip fruit in egg white. Remove, set aside to drain slightly, then coat with caster sugar. Stand on a wire rack to dry for 2 hours or until set. Frosted fruit is best used on the day you do it, but will keep for 12 hours in an airtight container.

You can also crystallise miniature roses, rose petals and mint leaves using this method.

CHOCOLATE

Chocolate curls and shavings: Can be made by running a vegetable peeler down the side of a block of chocolate. If the chocolate is cold you will get shavings, if at room temperature, curls.

Chocolate caraques: Are made by spreading a layer of melted chocolate over a marble, granite or ceramic work surface. Allow the chocolate to set at room temperature. Then, holding a metal pastry scraper or large knife at a 45° angle slowly push it along the work surface away from you to form chocolate into cylinders. If chocolate shavings form, then it is too cold and it is best to start again.

Chocolate leaves: Choose non-poisonous, fresh, stiff leaves with raised veins. Retain as much stem as possible. Wash leaves, then dry well on absorbent kitchen paper. Brush the underside of leaves with melted chocolate and allow to set at room temperature. When set, carefully peel away leaf. Use one leaf to decorate an individual dessert, or make a bunch and use to decorate a larger dessert or cake.

Piped chocolate decorations: Are quick and easy to make. Trace a simple design onto a sheet of paper. Tape a sheet of baking or greaseproof paper to your work surface and slide the drawings under the paper. Place melted chocolate into a paper or material piping bag and, following the tracings, pipe thin lines. Allow to set at room temperature and then carefully remove, using a metal spatula. If you are not going to use these decorations immediately, store them in an airtight container in a cool place.

QUICK DECORATING IDEAS

Flaked almonds, chopped nuts (such as pistachio, pecans and macadamia), and chopped or grated chocolate are all good for decorating the sides of cakes. Spread the sides with butter icing then roll them in your chosen decoration.

Try the following decorating suggestions:

- chocolate sprinkles
- hundreds and thousands
- chocolate thins
- warmed sieved jam
- glacé and dried fruits
- sifted icing sugar
- cinnamon sugar
- sugared violets
- crushed meringue
- sifted cocoa powder
- wafer biscuit rolls
- strawberries half dipped in chocolate

FEATHERED ICING

This technique is most effective if you use Glacé Icing. To make Glacé Icing, place 200 g/6¹/₂ oz sifted pure icing sugar in a bowl and beat in ¹/₃-¹/₂ cup (90-125 mL/ 3-4 fl oz) warm water to make an icing of spreadable consistency. Mix in ¹/₄ teaspoon vanilla essence. Glacé Icing should be used immediately. Before covering cake place 2 tablespoons of icing in a separate bowl and colour with a few drops of food colouring. Stand cake on a wire rack and pour over plain Glacé Icing. Place coloured icing in a piping bag and pipe thin straight lines across cake surface. Draw a skewer across the lines at 2 cm/ ³/₄ in intervals and then back in the opposite direction between the original lines. This technique works well for all shapes of cakes.

For a spider web effect on a round cake, start at the centre and pipe the icing in a spiral. Then, starting at the centre, divide the cake into eight portions by dragging a skewer out towards the edge. Finally divide the cake eight more times by dragging the skewer in the opposite direction between the original lines.

QUICK AND EASY

Easy and irresistible – the desserts
in this chapter are ideal for impromptu
gatherings or those times when you
need a sweet treat.

Top: Simple Elegance (see page 77)
Right: Chocolate Brownie Torte and
Ice Cream (recipe page 32)

Pink plates, cups and saucers Mosman Antique Centre

31

CHOCOLATE BROWNIE TORTE AND ICE CREAM

This flat dense brownie is ready to eat in less than half an hour.

Serves 6
Oven temperature 180°C, 350°F, Gas 4

- [ ] **185 g/6 oz dark chocolate, roughly chopped**
- [ ] **45 g/1¹/₂ oz butter, chopped**
- [ ] **1 egg**
- [ ] **¹/₄ cup/60 g/2 oz caster sugar**
- [ ] **¹/₂ teaspoon vanilla essence**
- [ ] **30 g/1 oz flour**
- [ ] **60 g/2 oz slivered almonds**
- [ ] **6 scoops ice cream, flavour of your choice**

1   Place 125 g/4 oz chocolate and butter in a heatproof bowl over a saucepan of simmering water and heat, stirring, for 5 minutes or until chocolate melts and mixture is smooth.

2   Place egg, sugar and vanilla essence in a bowl and beat until mixture is thick and creamy. Beat in chocolate mixture, then fold in flour, almonds and remaining chocolate pieces. Spoon mixture into a lightly greased and lined 20 cm/8 in sandwich tin and bake for 15-20 minutes or until cooked when tested with a skewer. Turn onto a wire rack to cool for 5-10 minutes before serving.

Serving suggestion: Cut brownie into wedges and serve warm accompanied by a scoop of ice cream – coffee-flavoured ice cream is a delicious accompaniment for this dessert.

DATES WITH ORANGE FILLING

Serves 4

- [ ] **315 g/10 oz fresh dates**
- [ ] **¹/₄ cup/60 mL/2 fl oz cognac or brandy**
- [ ] **¹/₄ teaspoon ground cinnamon**
- [ ] **¹/₄ teaspoon ground cardamom**
- [ ] **1 orange, sliced**
- [ ] **fine strips orange rind**

ORANGE FILLING
- [ ] **125 g/4 oz mascarpone**
- [ ] **4 teaspoons icing sugar**
- [ ] **2 teaspoons finely grated orange rind**
- [ ] **4 teaspoons orange juice**

1   Remove seeds from dates, by cutting through centre of dates lengthways then opening them out. Place cognac or brandy, cinnamon and cardamom in a glass dish and mix to combine. Add dates and toss well to coat. Cover and set aside to macerate for 1 hour.

2   To make filling, place mascarpone, icing sugar, orange rind and juice in a mixing bowl and beat until light and fluffy. Spoon mascarpone mixture into a piping bag fitted with a medium-sized fluted nozzle.

3   Remove dates from cognac mixture using a slotted spoon. Pat dry with absorbent kitchen paper, then pipe mascarpone mixture into the centre of each date. Refrigerate until required.

Serving suggestions: Serve with halved orange slices and rind strips. These dates may be served as an after-dinner treat accompanied by a cup of rich coffee.

Variation: In place of the mascarpone in this recipe you can use a mixture of cream cheese and cream. Beat 60 g/2 oz softened cream cheese until smooth, then whip ¹/₄ cup/60 mL/2 fl oz cream (double) until soft peaks form. Fold whipped cream into cream cheese and stir in icing sugar, orange rind and juice.

ROCKY ROAD ICE CREAM

Serves 6

- [ ] **1 litre/1³/₄ pt vanilla ice cream, softened**
- [ ] **2 x 60 g/2 oz chocolate-coated Turkish delight bars, chopped**
- [ ] **10 pink marshmallows, chopped**
- [ ] **5 white marshmallows, chopped**
- [ ] **6 red glacé cherries, chopped**
- [ ] **6 green glacé cherries, chopped**
- [ ] **4 tablespoons shredded coconut, toasted**
- [ ] **2 x 45 g/1¹/₂ oz chocolate-coated scorched peanut bars, chopped**

Place ice cream in a large mixing bowl, fold in Turkish delight, pink and white marshmallows, red and green cherries, coconut and peanut bars. Spoon mixture into a freezerproof container, cover and freeze until firm.

Serving suggestion: Place scoops of ice cream into bowls and serve with wafers.

Blue plate and napkin The Baytree Kitchen Shop

Dates with Orange Filling, Rocky Road Ice Cream, Yogurt and Orange Pancakes

YOGURT AND ORANGE PANCAKES

Pancakes, one of the quickest desserts you can make, can be prepared ahead of time then reheated prior to serving.

Serves 4

- ☐ **1 cup/125 g/4 oz flour**
- ☐ **¹/₂ teaspoon salt**
- ☐ **¹/₂ teaspoon bicarbonate of soda**
- ☐ **1¹/₄ cups/250 g/8 oz natural yogurt**
- ☐ **1 egg, lightly beaten**
- ☐ **¹/₃ cup/90 mL/3 fl oz milk**

ORANGE COINTREAU SAUCE
- ☐ **1 teaspoon finely grated orange rind**
- ☐ **¹/₂ cup/125 mL/4 fl oz orange juice**
- ☐ **2 tablespoons caster sugar**
- ☐ **1 teaspoon cornflour blended with 2 teaspoons water**
- ☐ **2 tablespoons Cointreau (orange liqueur)**

1   Sift together flour, salt and bicarbonate of soda into a mixing bowl. Make a well in the centre of the flour mixture. Combine yogurt, egg and milk and mix into flour mixture until ingredients are just combined.

2   Drop spoonfuls of mixture into a lightly greased, heavy-based frying pan and cook until bubbles form on the surface, then turn pancakes and cook on other side until golden.

3   To make sauce, place orange rind, juice and sugar in a saucepan and cook over a medium heat, stirring constantly, until sugar dissolves. Stir in cornflour mixture and cook for 1-2 minutes longer or until sauce thickens. Stir in Cointreau and heat for 1-2 minutes longer.

Serving suggestion: Top pancakes with sauce and accompany with natural yogurt.

STUFFED LYCHEES WITH BERRY SABAYON

Serves 6

- ☐ **48 lychees, peeled**
- ☐ **200 g/6¹/₂ oz blueberries**

BERRY SABAYON
- ☐ **4 egg yolks**
- ☐ **¹/₃ cup/75 g/2¹/₂ oz caster sugar**
- ☐ **100 g/3¹/₂ oz mixed berries, puréed and sieved**

1   To remove seed from lychees, cut flesh away from top of seed and gently pull seed away from flesh. Stuff each lychee with a blueberry.

2   To make sabayon, place egg yolks and sugar in a large heatproof bowl over a saucepan of simmering water. Beat mixture for 5-10 minutes or until thick and fluffy. Fold in puréed berries. Place lychees in serving bowls and top with sabayon. Decorate with remaining blueberries.

Variation: You might like to use redcurrants in place of the blueberries for this recipe.

CHOCOLATE BERRY MILLEFEUILLES

Serves 6
Oven temperature as per packet

- ☐ **1 packet chocolate cake mix**
- ☐ **250 g/8 oz blueberries**
- ☐ **250 g/8 oz raspberries**
- ☐ **2 tablespoons icing sugar**

CHOCOLATE CREAM
- ☐ **1 cup/250 mL/8 fl oz cream (double), whipped**
- ☐ **155 g/5 oz milk chocolate, melted and cooled**
- ☐ **2 tablespoons brandy**

1   Prepare chocolate cake following packet directions. Divide batter between two greased and lined 26 x 32 cm/10¹/₂ x 12³/₄ in Swiss roll tins and bake for 8-10 minutes or until cooked when tested with a skewer. Turn onto a wire rack to cool. Using a 7.5 cm/3 in round biscuit cutter cut out twelve rounds of cake.

2   To make Chocolate Cream, place cream in a bowl and fold in chocolate and brandy.

3   To assemble millefeuilles, spread each cake round with Chocolate Cream. Top six rounds with blueberries and six with raspberries, then sprinkle with icing sugar. Place a blueberry-topped round on a serving plate and top with a raspberry topped round. Just prior to serving sprinkle with remaining icing sugar.

Cook's tip: If blueberries are unavailable you can use just raspberries or any berries of your choice.

CREAMY FRUIT PARFAITS

Serves 6

- ☐ ⅓ cup/90 mL/3 fl oz white wine
- ☐ 1 tablespoon lime juice
- ☐ ¼ cup/60 g/2 oz sugar
- ☐ 1¼ cups/310 mL/10 fl oz cream (double)
- ☐ ⅓ cup/90 mL/3 fl oz mango purée
- ☐ 250 g/8 oz strawberries, hulled and sliced
- ☐ 2 kiwifruit, peeled and chopped
- ☐ 1 mango, peeled and thinly sliced

1   Place wine, lime juice and sugar in a saucepan and cook over a medium heat, stirring constantly, until sugar dissolves. Remove from heat and set aside to cool. Refrigerate until chilled.

2   Place cream, mango purée and wine mixture in a large mixing bowl and beat until soft peaks form.

3   Arrange a layer of mango slices in the base of four dessert glasses and top with a spoonful of mango cream. Continue layering using kiwifruit, strawberries and mango cream, finishing with mango cream. Refrigerate until required.

GINGERED PEAR CAKES

Serves 6
Oven temperature 180°C, 350°F, Gas 4

- ☐ ¼ cup/60 mL/2 fl oz vegetable oil
- ☐ ½ cup/125 g/4 oz muscovado or raw sugar
- ☐ 1 egg, lightly beaten
- ☐ 1 teaspoon vanilla essence
- ☐ 1 cup/125 g/4 oz flour
- ☐ 1 teaspoon bicarbonate of soda
- ☐ ½ teaspoon ground ginger
- ☐ ½ teaspoon ground nutmeg
- ☐ 2 pears, cored, peeled and finely diced
- ☐ 155 g/5 oz glacé ginger or stem ginger in syrup, chopped

GINGERED CREAM
- ☐ 1 cup/250 mL/8 fl oz cream (double),
- ☐ ¼ cup/60 g/2 oz sour cream
- ☐ 1 tablespoon honey
- ☐ 1 tablespoon brandy
- ☐ ¼ teaspoon ground ginger
- ☐ 1 tablespoon finely chopped glacé ginger or stem ginger in syrup

1   Place oil, sugar, egg and vanilla essence in a mixing bowl and beat to combine. Sift together flour, bicarbonate of soda, ginger and nutmeg. Mix flour mixture into egg mixture, then fold in pears and chopped ginger.

2   Spoon batter into six lightly greased large muffin tins and bake for 20 minutes. Reduce oven temperature to 160°C/325°F/ Gas 3 and cook for 15-20 minutes longer, or until cakes are cooked when tested with a skewer.

3   To make Gingered Cream, place cream, sour cream and honey in a mixing bowl and beat until soft peaks form. Add brandy and ground ginger and beat to combine, and until mixture stands in soft peaks. Fold in chopped ginger. Serve cakes hot or warm accompanied by Gingered Cream.

Left: Gingered Pear Cakes, Creamy Fruit Parfaits
Below: Stuffed Lychees with Berry Sabayon, Chocolate Berry Millefeuilles

Table Corso di Fiori Plates Accoutrement Cook Shop

merry
CHRISTMAS

Christmas is a time when food has a special significance. Whether you serve a Christmas Pudding or the traditional French Christmas Log it will be eagerly awaited at the end of the family meal.

FRENCH CHRISTMAS LOG

Serves 10
Oven temperature 180°C, 350°F, Gas 4

- [ ] **5 eggs**
- [ ] **¹/₂ cup/100 g/3¹/₂ oz caster sugar**
- [ ] **60 g/2 oz dark chocolate, melted and cooled**
- [ ] **¹/₂ cup/60 g/2 oz self-raising flour**
- [ ] **6 teaspoons cocoa powder**
- [ ] **icing sugar**

RUM FILLING
- [ ] **³/₄ cup/185 mL/6 fl oz cream (double)**
- [ ] **1 tablespoon icing sugar**
- [ ] **1 tablespoon dark rum**

GANACH ICING
- [ ] **185 g/6 oz dark chocolate**
- [ ] **²/₃ cup/170 mL/5¹/₂ fl oz cream (double)**
- [ ] **30 g/1 oz unsalted butter**

CHOCOLATE MUSHROOMS
- [ ] **1 egg white**
- [ ] **¹/₂ teaspoon vinegar**
- [ ] **¹/₃ cup/75 g/2¹/₂ oz caster sugar**
- [ ] **1 teaspoon cornflour**
- [ ] **30 g/1 oz dark chocolate, melted**
- [ ] **1 teaspoon cocoa powder**

1   Place eggs in a mixing bowl and beat until fluffy. Gradually add sugar, beating well after each addition, until thick and creamy. Beat in chocolate. Sift together flour and cocoa powder and fold into egg mixture. Pour mixture into a greased and lined 26 x 32 cm/10¹/₂ x 12³/₄ in Swiss roll tin and bake for 10-12 minutes or until just firm. Turn cake onto a damp teatowel dusted with cocoa powder, remove baking paper and roll up cake from short end. Allow to stand for 2-3 minutes, then unroll, cover with a second damp teatowel and set aside to cool.

2   To make filling, place cream, icing sugar and rum in a mixing bowl and beat until soft peaks form. Cover and chill until required.

3   To make icing, place chocolate, cream and butter in a saucepan and cook, stirring constantly, over a low heat until mixture is well combined. Remove from heat and chill until mixture is almost set, but of a spreadable consistency. Beat mixture until thick, then chill until required.

4   To make mushrooms, place egg white and vinegar in a small mixing bowl and beat until soft peaks form. Gradually add sugar, beating well after each addition, until mixture is thick and glossy. Fold in cornflour. Spoon mixture into a piping bag fitted with a plain nozzle and, onto a greased and lined baking tray, pipe seven button shapes for the tops of the mushrooms and small nobs for the stems. Reduce oven temperature to 120°C/250°F/Gas ¹/₂ and bake for 30 minutes or until meringue is crisp and dry. Allow meringues to cool on tray, then join tops and stems, using a little melted chocolate, to make mushrooms. Sprinkle with cocoa powder.

5   To assemble log, spread cake with filling and roll up. Spread log with icing and mark with a spatula to show textured bark. Decorate with mushrooms and dust with icing sugar.

Serving suggestion: Decorate serving plate with any remaining mushrooms. Cut into slices and serve with vanilla ice cream, if desired.

TRADITIONAL CHRISTMAS PUDDING

Serves 10-12

- [ ] **500 g/1 lb sultanas**
- [ ] **250 g/8 oz raisins**
- [ ] **60 g/2 oz mixed peel**
- [ ] **125 g/4 oz glacé apricots, chopped**
- [ ] **125 g/4 oz glacé cherries, halved**
- [ ] **125 g/4 oz blanched almonds**
- [ ] **³/₄ cup/185 mL/ 6 fl oz brandy**
- [ ] **250 g/8 oz butter, softened**
- [ ] **¹/₂ cup/90 g/3 oz brown sugar**
- [ ] **1 tablespoon finely grated orange rind**
- [ ] **4 eggs**
- [ ] **4 teaspoons freshly squeezed orange juice**
- [ ] **1 cup/125 g/4 oz flour**
- [ ] **1 teaspoon ground cinnamon**
- [ ] **¹/₂ teaspoon ground mixed spice**
- [ ] **¹/₂ teaspoon ground nutmeg**
- [ ] **4 cups/240 g/7¹/₂ oz bread crumbs made from stale bread**

1   Combine sultanas, raisins, mixed peel, apricots, cherries, almonds and brandy in a bowl and set aside.

2   Place butter, sugar and orange rind in a large mixing bowl and beat until creamy. Add eggs one at a time, beating well after each addition. Mix in orange juice.

3   Sift together flour, cinnamon, mixed spice and nutmeg. Fold flour mixture, fruit mixture and bread crumbs into butter mixture.

4   Spoon pudding mixture into an 8 cup/ 2 litre/3¹/₂ pt capacity pudding basin lined with an oven bag. Seal oven bag with string, place a piece of aluminium foil over pudding and seal with pudding basin lid. Place basin in a large saucepan with enough water to come halfway up the side of the basin. Boil for 4¹/₂-5¹/₂ hours or until pudding is cooked through. Serve hot, warm or cold with whipped cream or vanilla ice cream.

Cook's tip: If the pudding is not to be eaten immediately it may be stored in the refrigerator, wrapped in the oven bag, then reheated by reboiling in the pudding basin for 1 hour.

Traditional Christmas Pudding, French Christmas Log

Glasses Waterford Wedgwood

FABULOUS FAVOURITES

This chapter is filled with desserts that are loved around the world. Delight your family with a pavlova – the all-time favourite in Australia and New Zealand. Try your hand at an American angel food cake or the rich, smooth, creamy toffee-topped French crème brûlée. And who can resist the ever-popular English bread and butter pudding or fruit fritters.

Top: Bow Napkin (see page 76)
Right: The Perfect Pavlova
(recipe page 40)

baskets of BERRIES

Loganberries: A cross between the raspberry and blackberry, these pink-burgundy coloured berries were developed in 1881 in California. They are now cultivated in many temperate climates. Available fresh during midsummer, they are also available canned and may be used in place of raspberries or blackberries.

Blackberries: These late summer to early autumn fruit, cultivated on trellises in America, are still gathered wild from hedges in Europe and Australia. Berries should have a uniform dark colouring with a bright appearance. Blackberries are delicious eaten fresh, preserved or in a variety of hot or cold desserts.

Blueberries: A member of the heather family, this dark blue, small fruit is available in midsummer. Native to North America and East Asia, it is slightly tart and is popular in pies.

Boysenberries: The fruit of a trailing plant, the boysenberry is a cluster of purple-red droplets. Cultivated in America, Australia and New Zealand, it is available during summer. Available canned, they may be substituted for blackberries. Delicious in pies, tarts, frozen desserts, preserves, or just enjoyed with a sprinkling of sugar and freshly whipped cream.

Gooseberries: Enjoyed since the Middle Ages, these summer berries are native to Europe and North America. The sweeter varieties may be eaten with a sprinkling of sugar, while the more tart varieties are best made into preserves or used in desserts.

THE PERFECT PAVLOVA

Both Australia and New Zealand claim to have created this truly marvellous dessert. However, both agree that it is named after the famous Russian ballerina.

Serves 8
Oven temperature 120°C, 250°F, Gas ½

- ☐ 6 egg whites
- ☐ 1½ cups/315 g/10 oz caster sugar
- ☐ 6 teaspoons cornflour, sifted
- ☐ 1½ teaspoons white vinegar
- ☐ 315 mL/10 oz cream (double), whipped
- ☐ selection of fresh fruits, such as orange segments, sliced bananas, sliced peaches, passion fruit pulp, berries or sliced kiwifruit

1 Place egg whites in a mixing bowl and beat until soft peaks form. Gradually add sugar, beating well after each addition, until mixture is thick and glossy.

2 Fold cornflour and vinegar into egg white mixture. Grease a baking tray and line with nonstick baking paper. Grease paper and dust lightly with flour. Mark a 23 cm/9 in diameter circle on paper.

3 Place one-quarter of the egg white mixture in the centre of the circle and spread out to within 3 cm/1¼ in of the edge. Pile remaining mixture around edge of circle and neaten using a metal spatula or knife. Bake for 1½-2 hours or until firm to touch. Turn off oven and cool pavlova in oven with door ajar. Decorate cold pavlova with cream and top with fruit.

Cook's tip: You may like to add extra crunch by sprinkling the top of the pavlova with nuts.

BLACKBERRY CREME BRULEE

Blackberries hidden in the base of this rich, toffee-topped custard give a new twist to a classic recipe.

Serves 6

- ☐ 200 g/7½ oz blackberries
- ☐ 2 cups/500 mL/16 fl oz cream (double)
- ☐ 1 vanilla bean (pod)
- ☐ 5 egg yolks
- ☐ 1 cup/220 g/7 oz caster sugar

Table Corso di Fiori

40

TOFFEE TOPPING

- ☐ **½ cup/125 g/4 oz sugar**
- ☐ **¼ cup/60 mL/ 2 fl oz water**

1 Divide blackberries between six ½ cup/ 125 mL/4 fl oz capacity ramekins. Place cream and vanilla bean in a saucepan and bring to the boil. Place egg yolks and sugar in a bowl and beat until thick and creamy. Continue beating while slowly pouring in hot cream. Return mixture to saucepan and cook, stirring, over a low heat until mixture thickens. Remove vanilla bean. Pour cream mixture into ramekins and refrigerate until custards set.

2 To make topping, place sugar and water in a saucepan and cook, stirring, over a medium heat until sugar dissolves. Bring mixture to the boil and boil, without stirring, until sugar syrup is a medium brown colour. Swirl pan once or twice during cooking. Carefully spoon toffee over cold brûlées and set aside to harden.

Cook's tip: If blackberries are unavailable any berries can be used in their place. You might like to try a mixture of berries. Other fruits are also delicious prepared this way. If using fruits such as apricots or peaches they will need to be lightly poached first.

BERRY CHOCOLATE MUD CAKE

Chocolate and raspberries – what perfect partners. In this wonderful dessert the raspberries offset the richness of the chocolate cake.

Serves 10
Oven temperature 120°C, 250°F, Gas ½

- ☐ **250 g/8 oz butter, chopped**
- ☐ **315 g/10 oz dark chocolate**
- ☐ **5 eggs, separated**
- ☐ **2 tablespoons caster sugar**
- ☐ **¼ cup/30 g/1 oz self-raising flour, sifted**
- ☐ **250 g/8 oz raspberries**
- ☐ **whipped cream, for serving**

RASPBERRY COULIS
- ☐ **250 g/8 oz raspberries**
- ☐ **sugar to taste**

1 Place butter and chocolate in a heatproof bowl and place over a saucepan of simmering water. Heat, stirring, until chocolate melts and mixture is smooth. Remove bowl and set aside to cool slightly.

2 Beat egg yolks and sugar into chocolate mixture, then fold in flour.

3 Place egg whites in a bowl and beat until stiff peaks form. Fold egg whites and raspberries into chocolate mixture. Pour into a greased and lined 20 cm/8 in round cake tin. Bake for 1¼ hours or until cooked when tested with a skewer. Turn off oven and cool cake in oven with door ajar.

4 To make coulis, place raspberries in a food processor or blender and process until puréed. Push purée through a sieve to remove seeds. Add sugar to taste. Accompany cake with coulis and cream.

Berry Chocolate Mud Cake, Blackberry Crème Brûlée

41

The perfect angel food cake has a crisp crust and is light, puffy and cloud-like
The secret is to sift the ingredients a number of times to incorporate as
much air as possible and to have a light hand. This recipe with coconut
folded through the batter makes a magical dessert.

COCONUT ANGEL FOOD CAKE

Serves 12
Oven temperature 180°C, 350°F, Gas 4

- [ ] ³/₄ **cup/90 g/3 oz flour**
- [ ] ¹/₄ **cup/30 g/1 oz cornflour**
- [ ] **1 cup/220 g/7 oz caster sugar**
- [ ] **10 egg whites**
- [ ] ¹/₂ **teaspoon salt**
- [ ] **1 teaspoon cream of tartar**
- [ ] **8 teaspoons water**
- [ ] **1 teaspoon vanilla essence**
- [ ] **45 g/1¹/₂ oz shredded coconut**

FLUFFY FROSTING
- [ ] ¹/₂ **cup/125 mL/4 fl oz water**
- [ ] **1¹/₄ cups/315 g/10 oz sugar**
- [ ] **3 egg whites**
- [ ] **90 g/3 oz shredded coconut, lightly toasted**

1   Sift together flour and cornflour three times, then sift once more with ¹/₄ cup/60 g/ 2 oz of the sugar.

2   Place egg whites, salt, cream of tartar and water in a large mixing bowl and beat until stiff peaks form. Take care that you do not beat until the mixture is dry. Beat in vanilla essence, then fold in remaining sugar, 1 tablespoon at a time.

3   Sift flour mixture over egg white mixture then gently fold in. Lastly sprinkle coconut over top of batter and fold in. Spoon batter into an ungreased angel cake tin, then draw a spatula gently through the mixture to break up any large air pockets. Bake for 45 minutes. When cake is cooked invert tin and allow the cake to hang while it is cooling.

4   To make frosting, place water and sugar in a saucepan and cook over a medium heat, without boiling, stirring constantly until sugar dissolves. Brush any sugar from sides of tin using a pastry brush dipped in water. Bring the syrup to the boil

and boil rapidly for 3-5 minutes, without stirring, or until syrup reaches the soft-ball stage (115°C/239°F on a sweet thermometer). Place egg whites in a mixing bowl and beat until soft peaks form. Continue beating while pouring in syrup in a thin stream, a little at a time. Continue beating until all syrup is used and frosting stands in stiff peaks. Spread frosting over top and sides of cake and press toasted coconut onto sides of cake.

2   Spoon batter into an ungreased angel cake tin, then draw a spatula gently through the mixture to break up any large air pockets.

3   When cake is cooked, invert tin and allow the cake to hang while it is cooling.

Cook's tip: An angel cake tin is a deep-sided ring tin with a removable base that has a centre tube higher than the outside edges. If you do not have one of these tins you can use an ordinary deep-sided ring tin with a removable base. However, when you invert the tin for the cake to cool, place the tube over a funnel or bottle. Never grease an angel cake tin as this will stop the cake rising.

1   Place egg whites, salt, cream of tartar and water in a large mixing bowl and beat until stiff peaks form. Beat in vanilla essence, then fold in remaining sugar, 1 tablespoon at a time.

Table Malcolm Smith

43

Marble stand Corso di Fiori Cake server and napkin The Baytree Kitchen Shop

DEVIL'S FOOD CAKE

Serves 12
Oven temperature 180°C, 350°F, Gas 4

- ☐ **1 cup/100 g/3¹/₂ oz cocoa powder**
- ☐ **1¹/₂ cups/375 mL/12 fl oz boiling water**
- ☐ **375 g/12 oz unsalted butter, softened**
- ☐ **1 teaspoon vanilla essence**
- ☐ **1¹/₂ cups/315 g/10 oz caster sugar**
- ☐ **4 eggs**
- ☐ **2¹/₂ cups/315 g/10 oz flour**
- ☐ **¹/₂ cup/60 g/2 oz cornflour**
- ☐ **1 teaspoon bicarbonate of soda**
- ☐ **1 teaspoon salt**
- ☐ **¹/₂ cup/125 mL/4 fl oz cream (double), whipped**

CHOCOLATE BUTTER ICING
- ☐ **250 g/8 oz butter, softened**
- ☐ **1 egg**
- ☐ **2 egg yolks**
- ☐ **1 cup/155 g/5 oz icing sugar, sifted**
- ☐ **185 g/6 oz dark chocolate, melted and cooled**

1   Combine cocoa powder and water in a small bowl and mix until blended. Set aside to cool. Place butter and vanilla essence in a large mixing bowl and beat until light and fluffy. Gradually add sugar, beating well after each addition until mixture is creamy. Beat in eggs one at a time, beating well after each addition.

2   Sift together flour, cornflour, bicarbonate of soda and salt into a bowl. Fold flour mixture and cocoa mixture, alternately, into egg mixture.

3   Divide batter between three greased and lined 23 cm/9 in sandwich tins and bake for 20-25 minutes or until cakes are cooked when tested with a skewer. Stand in tins for 5 minutes before turning onto wire racks to cool completely.

4   To make icing, place butter in a mixing bowl and beat until light and fluffy. Mix in egg, egg yolks and icing sugar. Add chocolate and beat until icing is thick and creamy. Sandwich cakes together using whipped cream then cover top and sides with butter icing.

LEMON SULTANA CHEESECAKE

The tangy taste of lemon combines with cream cheese and yogurt to make this irresistible cheesecake.

Serves 8
Oven temperature 220°C, 425°F, Gas 7

PASTRY
- ☐ ½ cup/60 g/2 oz flour
- ☐ ¼ cup/30 g/1 oz cornflour
- ☐ ¼ cup/30 g/1 oz custard powder
- ☐ 4 teaspoons icing sugar
- ☐ 60 g/2 oz butter
- ☐ 1 egg yolk
- ☐ iced water

CHEESECAKE FILLING
- ☐ 375 g/12 oz cream cheese, softened
- ☐ ¼ cup/45 g/1½ oz natural yogurt
- ☐ ½ cup/100 g/3½ oz caster sugar
- ☐ 2 eggs
- ☐ 1 teaspoon vanilla essence
- ☐ 2 teaspoons finely grated lemon rind
- ☐ 170 g/5½ oz sultanas

LEMON TOPPING
- ☐ ½ cup/125 mL/4 fl oz cream (double)
- ☐ 2 teaspoons lemon juice
- ☐ ½ teaspoon finely grated lemon rind

1 To make pastry, sift together flour, cornflour, custard powder and icing sugar into a large mixing bowl. Rub in butter with fingertips until mixture resembles coarse bread crumbs. Make a well in the centre of the mixture and stir in egg yolk and enough water to make a firm dough. Wrap in plastic food wrap and refrigerate for 30 minutes.

2 Roll out pastry to fit the base of a greased 20 cm/8 in springform tin. Using a fork, prick pastry base and bake for 10 minutes. Set aside to cool.

3 To make filling, place cream cheese, yogurt, sugar, eggs, vanilla essence and lemon rind in a mixing bowl and beat until smooth. Fold in sultanas. Spoon mixture into prepared cake tin. Reduce oven temperature to 180°C/350°F/Gas 4 and bake for 20-25 minutes or until firm. Turn off oven and leave cheesecake to cool in oven with door ajar.

4 To make topping, place cream, lemon juice and rind in a small saucepan and bring to simmering, then simmer, stirring, for 5 minutes or until mixture thickens. Pour topping over cooled cheesecake and chill until required.

Left: Lemon Sultana Cheesecake
Below: Devil's Food Cake

Plate Villeroy and Boch

BANANA FRITTERS WITH CARAMEL SAUCE

Fruit fritters are always popular, especially with children. You might like to make these using other fruits, such as apples, peaches or canned pineapple rings.

Serves 4

- [ ] **4 large firm bananas, cut in half then split lengthways**
- [ ] **2 tablespoons lime juice**
- [ ] **oil for cooking**

BATTER
- [ ] **1 cup/125 g/4 oz self-raising flour, sifted**
- [ ] **1 egg, lightly beaten**
- [ ] **1/2 cup/125 mL/4 fl oz milk**
- [ ] **2 tablespoons caster sugar**
- [ ] **1 egg white**

CARAMEL SAUCE
- [ ] **1/2 cup/125 g/4 oz sugar**
- [ ] **1/2 cup/125 mL/4 fl oz water**
- [ ] **1/2 cup/125 mL/4 fl oz cream (double)**
- [ ] **2 teaspoons whisky (optional)**

1   To make batter, place flour in a mixing bowl and make a well in the centre. Combine egg, milk and sugar and mix into flour mixture to make a batter of a smooth consistency. Set aside to stand for 10 minutes.

2   To make sauce, place sugar and water in a saucepan and cook over a low heat, stirring constantly, until sugar dissolves. Bring to the boil, then reduce heat and simmer, without stirring, for 5 minutes or until mixture is golden.

3   Remove pan from heat and carefully stir in cream and whisky, if using. Return pan to a low heat and cook, stirring carefully, until combined. Remove pan from heat and set aside to cool.

4   Beat egg white until soft peaks form, then fold into batter. Heat oil in a large saucepan. Brush bananas with lime juice and dip in batter to coat. Drain off excess batter and cook bananas in hot oil for 2-3 minutes or until golden. Drain on absorbent kitchen paper. Serve immediately with sauce.

Glasses, plates Waterford Wedgwood Soufflé dish Mikasa Tableware Material Potter Williams

46

FRUITY BREAD AND BUTTER PUDDING

The fruitiest bread and butter pudding you will ever have. This version of the traditional English pudding uses sultanas, apples and fruit loaf to make it extra fruity.

Serves 8
Oven temperature 180°C, 350°F, Gas 4

- ☐ **60 g/2 oz butter**
- ☐ **¹/₂ cup/90 g/3 oz brown sugar**
- ☐ **90 g/3 oz sultanas**
- ☐ **¹/₂ teaspoon ground cinnamon**
- ☐ **440 g/14 oz canned sliced apples**
- ☐ **12 thick slices fruit loaf, buttered and crusts removed**
- ☐ **3 eggs**
- ☐ **1¹/₄ cups/310 mL/10 fl oz milk**
- ☐ **³/₄ cup/185 mL/6 fl oz cream (double)**
- ☐ **¹/₂ teaspoon vanilla essence**

1   Melt butter in a frying pan and add sugar and cook, stirring constantly, over a medium heat until sugar dissolves. Stir in sultanas, cinnamon and apples, toss to combine and cook for 1-2 minutes longer. Remove pan from heat and set aside to cool.

2   Cut bread slices into triangles and arrange one-third, buttered side up, in the base of a greased ovenproof dish. Top with half the apple mixture and another layer of bread triangles. Spoon over remaining apple mixture and top with bread triangles and arrange remaining slices around the edges.

3   Place eggs, milk, cream and vanilla in a mixing bowl and beat until well combined. Pour carefully over bread and apples in dish. Place dish in a baking dish with enough water to come halfway up the sides of ovenproof dish. Bake for 45-50 minutes or until pudding is firm and top is golden.

JAFFA SELF-SAUCING PUDDING

Chocolate and orange combine in this recipe to make the most wonderful self-saucing pudding you will ever taste.

Serves 8
Oven temperature 180°C, 350°F, Gas 4

- ☐ **125 g/4 oz butter**
- ☐ **2 teaspoons finely grated orange rind**
- ☐ **³/₄ cup/170 g/5¹/₂ oz caster sugar**
- ☐ **2 eggs**
- ☐ **100 g/3¹/₂ oz chocolate chips**
- ☐ **1¹/₂ cups/185 g/6 oz self-raising flour, sifted**
- ☐ **¹/₂ cup/125 mL/4 fl oz orange juice**
- ☐ **¹/₄ cup/30 g/1 oz cocoa powder**
- ☐ **¹/₂ cup/100 g/3¹/₂ oz caster sugar**
- ☐ **1¹/₂ cups/375 mL/12 fl oz boiling water**

1   Place butter and orange rind in a large mixing bowl and beat until light and fluffy. Gradually add sugar, beating well after each addition until mixture is creamy.

2   Beat in eggs one at a time. Toss chocolate chips in flour, then fold flour mixture and orange juice, alternately, into batter. Spoon batter into a greased ovenproof dish.

3   Sift together cocoa powder and sugar over batter in dish, then carefully add boiling water. Bake for 40 minutes or until pudding is firm.

Fruity Bread and Butter Pudding,
Banana Fritters with Caramel Sauce,
Jaffa Self-Saucing Pudding

LIGHT AND LOW
delights

Low in calories and light in texture, these sinfully delicious desserts are hardly wicked at all. Peach and Apple Soufflé tastes wonderful and you would never guess that it has no cholesterol, almost no fat and fewer than 100 calories a serve. Even if you are not on a diet, these desserts make the perfect finish.

Top: Simple Elegance (see page 77)
Right: Coeur à la Crème with Fresh
Fruits (recipe page 50)

COEUR A LA CREME
WITH FRESH FRUITS

*Start preparing this dessert the day
before serving as it has to sit in
the refrigerator overnight.*

Serves 4

- ☐ ²/₃ **cup/185 g/6 oz cottage cheese**
- ☐ ¹/₄ **cup/60 mL/2 fl oz cream (double)**
- ☐ ¹/₄ **cup/60 g/2 oz reduced-fat cream cheese**
- ☐ **1 tablespoon icing sugar**
- ☐ ¹/₂ **teaspoon vanilla essence**
- ☐ **1 tablespoon Cointreau or Grand Marnier (orange liqueur)**
- ☐ **250 g/8 oz mixed fruits, such as berries of your choice, plums, peaches or melons**

1 Place cottage cheese in a food processor or blender and process until smooth. Add cream, cream cheese, icing sugar and vanilla essence and process until completely combined.

2 Line four coeur à la crème moulds with a double thickness of damp muslin or gauze and pack cheese mixture into moulds. Place moulds on a wire rack, on a tray. Cover and refrigerate for 24 hours. Turn crèmes onto serving plates, sprinkle each with a little Cointreau or Grand Marnier and garnish with fruit.

Coeur à la crème moulds: These are china, heart-shaped moulds with draining holes in the base. Before lining with the muslin you should rinse them in cold water, but do not dry. You can make your own moulds, using empty yogurt containers. Cut the containers down to make sides of about 2.5 cm/1 in, then, using a skewer, punch holes in the base. These moulds will not be heart-shaped like the traditional ones but the dessert will still look and taste wonderful.

PEACH AND
APPLE SOUFFLES

Serves 4
Oven temperature 180°C, 350°F, Gas 4

- ☐ **1 peach, peeled, stoned and chopped**
- ☐ **1 apple, cored, peeled and chopped**
- ☐ **1 teaspoon lemon juice**
- ☐ **4 teaspoons water**
- ☐ **4 teaspoons caster sugar**
- ☐ ¹/₂ **teaspoon vanilla essence**
- ☐ **4 egg whites**
- ☐ **1 tablespoon icing sugar, sifted**

1 Place peach, apple, lemon juice and water in a small saucepan and cook over a medium heat, covered, for 10 minutes or until fruit is soft.

2 Place fruit mixture in a food processor or blender and process until smooth. Return to pan, stir in 1¹/₂ teaspoons sugar and cook over a low heat, for 2 minutes longer to evaporate a little of the moisture. Stir in vanilla essence and set aside to cool.

3 Beat egg whites until soft peaks form, add remaining sugar and beat until stiff peaks form. Fold egg white mixture into fruit purée. Spoon mixture into four lightly greased soufflé dishes, place on a baking tray and cook for 12-15 minutes or until well puffed. Dust with icing sugar and serve immediately.

FRUIT COMPOTE

Serves 4

- ☐ **6 firm ripe peaches, halved and stones removed**
- ☐ **1 cup/250 mL/8 fl oz red wine**
- ☐ **2-3 tablespoons honey**
- ☐ **1 cinnamon stick**

Cut peaches into thick slices. Place wine, honey and cinnamon stick into a saucepan and bring to the boil, reduce heat and simmer for 5 minutes. Add peaches and cook for 5-10 minutes or until slightly softened. Set aside to cool, then chill.

Serving suggestion: Accompany with natural yogurt.

*Above: Peach and Apple Soufflés
Right: Fruit Compote, Raspberry and
Hazelnut Tarts*

RASPBERRY AND HAZELNUT TARTS

Any berries such as strawberries, blueberries or blackberries can be used to make these divine individual tarts.

Serves 6
Oven temperature 200°C, 400°F, Gas 6

HAZELNUT PASTRY
- ☐ **1 cup/125 g/4 oz flour, sifted**
- ☐ **1 tablespoon icing sugar**
- ☐ **30 g/1 oz hazelnuts, ground**
- ☐ **60 g/2 oz unsalted butter, chopped**
- ☐ **1 egg, lightly beaten**
- ☐ **1 egg yolk, lightly beaten**

CREAM FILLING
- ☐ **1¹⁄₂ cups/375 g/12 oz reduced-fat cream cheese**
- ☐ **2 tablespoons caster sugar**
- ☐ **¹⁄₄ cup/60 mL/2 fl oz cream (double)**

RASPBERRY TOPPING
- ☐ **350 g/11 oz raspberries**
- ☐ **¹⁄₃ cup/100 g/3¹⁄₂ oz raspberry jam, warmed and sieved**

1 To make pastry, place flour, icing sugar and hazelnuts in a bowl and mix to combine. Rub in butter, using fingertips, until mixture resembles fine bread crumbs. Add egg and egg yolk, and mix to form a soft dough. Wrap dough in plastic food wrap and refrigerate for 1 hour.

2 Knead pastry lightly, then roll out to 3 mm/¹⁄₈ in thick and line six lightly greased 7¹⁄₂ cm/3 in flan tins. Line pastry cases with baking paper and weigh down with uncooked rice and bake for 10 minutes. Remove paper and rice and bake for 15 minutes longer or until golden. Set aside to cool.

3 To make filling, place cream cheese, and sugar in a bowl and beat until smooth. Beat cream until soft peaks form, then fold into cream cheese mixture. Cover and chill for 20 minutes.

4 To assemble, spoon filling into pastry cases and smooth tops. Arrange raspberries over top of tarts, then brush warm jam over raspberries and refrigerate for a few minutes to set glaze.

Plates Villeroy & Boch Marble stand Corso di Fiori

RHUBARB FOOL WITH ORANGE BISCUITS

Serves 8
Oven temperature 190°C, 375°F, Gas 5

- ☐ **750 g/1¹/₂ lb rhubarb, trimmed and cut into 1 cm/¹/₂ in pieces**
- ☐ **1 cup/250 g/8 oz brown sugar**
- ☐ **¹/₄ teaspoon ground cloves**
- ☐ **¹/₂ teaspoon vanilla essence**
- ☐ **2 tablespoons lemon juice**
- ☐ **2 tablespoons orange juice**
- ☐ **³/₄ cup/185 mL/6 fl oz cream (doubie)**
- ☐ **¹/₂ cup/100 g/3¹/₂ oz natural yogurt**

ORANGE BISCUITS
- ☐ **75 g unsalted butter**
- ☐ **¹/₄ cup/60 g/2 oz caster sugar**
- ☐ **1 egg**
- ☐ **1¹/₂ teaspoons finely grated orange rind**
- ☐ **³/₄ cup/90 g/3 oz flour**

1   Place rhubarb, sugar, cloves, vanilla essence and lemon and orange juices in a saucepan. Bring to the boil, then reduce heat and simmer, stirring occasionally, for 15 minutes or until rhubarb is soft and mixture thick. Spoon rhubarb mixture into a bowl, cover and chill.

2   Place cream in a bowl and beat until soft peaks form. Fold yogurt into cream, then fold in chilled rhubarb mixture to give a marbled effect. Spoon into individual serving glasses and chill.

3   To make biscuits, place butter and sugar in a mixing bowl and beat until light and creamy. Add egg and orange rind and beat well to combine. Stir in flour.

4   Place teaspoons of mixture, 5 cm/2 in apart, on a lightly greased baking tray and bake for 10 minutes or until golden. Cool biscuits on trays for 1 minute before removing to wire racks to cool completely. Accompany each fool with two or three biscuits.

Table Made Where Glasses Waterford Wedgwood Glass vase Corso di Fiori

APPLE PUDDING WITH RICOTTA CREAM

The Ricotta Cream served with this pudding is a delicious alternative to cream. You might like to try it as an accompaniment to other desserts.

Serves 4
Oven temperature 200°C, 400°F, Gas 6

- ☐ **6 green apples, cored, peeled and cut into 1 cm/¹/₂ in slices**
- ☐ **100 g/3¹/₂ oz raisins**
- ☐ **60 g/2 oz pine nuts, toasted**
- ☐ **1 cup/250 mL/8 fl oz orange juice**

Plate Limoges

INDIVIDUAL SUMMER PUDDINGS

Fresh or frozen berries can be used to make this dessert.

Serves 4

- ☐ ½ cup/100 g/3½ oz caster sugar
- ☐ 2 cups/500 mL/16 fl oz water
- ☐ 875 g/1¾ lb mixed berries, such as raspberries, strawberries, blueberries or blackberries
- ☐ 14 slices bread, crusts removed

BERRY SAUCE
- ☐ 155 g/5 oz mixed berries, such as raspberries, strawberries, blueberries or blackberries
- ☐ 2 tablespoons icing sugar
- ☐ 1 tablespoon fresh lemon juice
- ☐ 2 tablespoons water

1   Place sugar and water in a saucepan and cook over a low heat, stirring constantly, until sugar dissolves. Bring to the boil, reduce heat, add berries and simmer for 4-5 minutes or until fruit is soft, but still retains its shape. Remove from heat. Drain, reserving liquid, and set aside to cool.

2   Cut 8 circles of bread with a pastry cutter. Line the base of four ½ cup/125 mL/4 fl oz capacity ramekins with 4 rounds of the bread. Cut remaining bread slices into fingers and line the sides of ramekins, trimming bread to fit if necessary. Spoon fruit into ramekins and enough reserved liquid to moisten bread well, then cover with remaining bread circles. Reserve any remaining liquid. Cover tops of ramekins with aluminium foil, top with a weight, and refrigerate overnight.

3   To make sauce, place berries, icing sugar, lemon juice and water in a food processor or blender and process until puréed. Push mixture through a sieve to remove seeds and chill until required.

4   Turn puddings onto individual serving plates, spoon sauce over or pass separately.

Serving suggestion: Garnish with additional berries and natural yogurt.

- ☐ ¼ cup/90 g/3 oz honey
- ☐ ½ teaspoon ground cinnamon
- ☐ 6 whole cloves
- ☐ 1 tablespoon finely grated orange rind
- ☐ 60 g/2 oz ground almonds

RICOTTA CREAM
- ☐ 100 g/3½ oz fresh ricotta cheese
- ☐ 100 g/3½ oz cottage cheese
- ☐ 1-2 tablespoons milk
- ☐ 1-2 tablespoons caster sugar

1   Layer apples, raisins and pine nuts in a shallow ovenproof dish. Pour over orange juice, drizzle with honey, then sprinkle with cinnamon, cloves, orange rind and almonds. Cover dish with aluminium foil and bake for 35-40 minutes or until apples are tender.

2   To make cream, place ricotta and cottage cheese in a food processor or blender and process until smooth. Add a little milk if the mixture is too thick and sweeten with sugar to taste.

Serving suggestion: Serve this dessert hot or cold with a little Ricotta Cream.

Left: Individual Summer Puddings
Above: Rhubarb Fool with Orange Biscuits, Apple Pudding with Ricotta Cream,

Carafe and glasses Villeroy & Boch *Plates* Waterford Wedgwood *Napkin* Baytree Kitchen Shop

SOMETHING SPECTACULAR

For a special occasion, a fabulous
home-cooked dinner followed by a spectacular
dessert is the perfect way to celebrate. Some of the
desserts in this section are quick and easy, while others
take a little more time to prepare, but are well worth
the effort. Try the Austrian Coffee Cake when
you want to impress, but time is short.

Top: Bow Napkin (see page 76)
Left: Layered Orange and Almond
Gâteau (recipe page 56)

LAYERED ORANGE AND ALMOND GATEAU

Serves 10
Oven temperature 180°C, 350°F, Gas 4

- ☐ **3 eggs**
- ☐ **1 cup/220 g/7 oz caster sugar**
- ☐ **4 teaspoons orange juice**
- ☐ **1 tablespoon finely grated orange rind**
- ☐ **1³/₄ cups/220 g/7 oz flour**
- ☐ **¹/₄ cup/30 g/1 oz cornflour**
- ☐ **1¹/₂ teaspoons baking powder**
- ☐ **1 teaspoon bicarbonate of soda**
- ☐ **250 g/8 oz sour cream, lightly beaten**
- ☐ **250 g/8 oz butter, melted and cooled**

GRAND MARNIER SYRUP
- ☐ **¹/₂ cup/125 g/4 oz sugar**
- ☐ **¹/₄ cup/60 mL/2 fl oz orange juice**
- ☐ **¹/₄ cup/60 mL/2 fl oz Grand Marnier (orange liqueur)**

ORANGE BUTTER CREAM
- ☐ **¹/₂ cup/125 g/4 oz sugar**
- ☐ **¹/₂ cup/125 mL/4 fl oz water**
- ☐ **4 egg yolks**
- ☐ **250 g/8 oz unsalted butter**
- ☐ **2 teaspoons finely grated orange rind**
- ☐ **¹/₄ cup/60 mL/2 fl oz orange juice**
- ☐ **2 tablespoons Grand Marnier**
- ☐ **75 g/2¹/₂ oz flaked almonds, toasted**

1   Place eggs, sugar, orange juice and rind in a large mixing bowl and beat until thick and creamy. Sift together flour, cornflour, baking powder and bicarbonate of soda. Place sour cream and butter in a small bowl and whisk lightly to combine. Fold flour and sour cream mixtures, alternately, into egg mixture.

2   Spoon batter into three lightly greased and lined 23 cm/9 in sandwich tins and bake for 15-20 minutes or until cooked when tested with a skewer.

3   To make syrup: Five minutes before cakes complete cooking, place sugar, orange juice and Grand Marnier in a saucepan and cook, stirring constantly, until sugar dissolves.

4   Turn cakes onto wire racks and, using a skewer, pierce surface of cakes to make holes that reach about halfway through the cakes. Spoon hot syrup over hot cakes and set aside to cool completely.

5   To make butter cream, place sugar and water in a small saucepan and cook,

Table Corso di Fiori Plate Accoutrement Cook Shop

over a medium heat, stirring constantly, until sugar dissolves. Bring syrup to the boil and cook until mixture reaches soft-ball stage (115°C/239°F on a sugar thermometer). Beat egg yolks to combine and continue beating while slowly pouring in sugar syrup. Beat for 5 minutes longer or until mixture cools and is of a thick mousse-like consistency. In a separate bowl beat butter until light and creamy, then gradually beat into egg yolk mixture. Beat in orange rind, juice and Grand Marnier.

6 To assemble, sandwich cakes together with a little butter cream, then spread remaining butter cream over top and sides of cake. Press almonds around sides of cake.

STRAWBERRY SHORTBREAD FAN

Serves 12
Oven temperature 180°C, 350°F, Gas 4

☐ **12 strawberries, halved**

SPONGE BASE
☐ **2 eggs**
☐ **¹/₂ cup/100 g/3¹/₂ oz caster sugar**
☐ **¹/₄ cup/60 mL/2 fl oz milk, warmed**
☐ **1 teaspoon butter, melted**
☐ **¹/₂ cup/60 g/2 oz flour, sifted**

SHORTBREAD
☐ **1 cup/125 g/4 oz flour, sifted**
☐ **30 g/1 oz icing sugar, sifted**
☐ **30 g/1 oz ground rice, sifted**
☐ **125 g/4 oz butter, cubed**
☐ **¹/₂ teaspoon finely grated lemon rind**
☐ **¹/₂ teaspoon vanilla essence**
☐ **100 g/3¹/₂ oz dark chocolate melted**

CREME PATISSIERE
☐ **1 egg**
☐ **2 egg yolks**
☐ **4 teaspoons flour, sifted**
☐ **4 teaspoons cornflour, sifted**
☐ **¹/₄ cup/60 g/2 oz caster sugar**
☐ **1 teaspoon vanilla essence**
☐ **1¹/₄ cups/310 mL/10 fl oz milk, scalded**
☐ **¹/₂ cup/125 mL/4 fl oz cream (double), whipped**

STRAWBERRY COULIS
☐ **250 g/8 oz strawberries, hulled and halved**
☐ **sugar to taste**

1 To make sponge, place eggs in a mixing bowl and beat until light and fluffy. Add

Cake servers Waterford Wedgwood

sugar a little at a time, beating well after each addition, until mixture is thick and creamy. Combine milk and butter. Fold flour and milk mixture, alternately, into egg mixture. Pour into a greased and lightly floured 20 cm/8 in round cake tin. Bake for 20-25 minutes or until cooked when tested with a skewer. Stand in tin for 5 minutes before turning onto a wire rack to cool completely.

2 To make Shortbread, combine flour, icing sugar and ground rice in a large mixing bowl. Rub in butter, using fingertips, until mixture resembles coarse bread crumbs. Stir in lemon rind and vanilla essence. Turn dough onto a floured surface and knead until dough is smooth. Roll out to 5 mm/¹/₄ in thick and, using a 20 cm/8 in round cake tin as a guide, cut out a circle. Place on a greased baking tray lined with nonstick baking paper. Mark twelve wedges on shortbread and cook at 160°C/325°F/Gas 3 for 40 minutes or until lightly browned. Cut into wedges and set aside to cool on tray.

3 Spread one side of each wedge with chocolate and set aside until chocolate sets.

4 To make Crème Pâtissière, place egg, egg yolks, flour, cornflour, sugar and vanilla essence in a small bowl and whisk to combine. Stir 2 tablespoons of hot milk into egg mixture, then stir mixture into remaining milk and cook, over a low heat, stirring constantly, until custard thickens. Set aside to cool. Fold in whipped cream.

5 To make coulis, place strawberries in a food processor or blender and process until smooth. Add sugar to taste.

6 To assemble, spread sponge with Crème Pâtissière and arrange shortbread wedges, angled upwards, on sponge with halved strawberries tucked between each wedge. Accompany cake with coulis.

Left: Strawberry Shortbread Fan
Above: Austrian Coffee Cake
(recipe page 58)

FRESH BERRY TART

You can use a combination of cream cheese and cream in place of the mascarpone in this recipe if you wish.

Serves 8
Oven temperature 200°C, 400°F, Gas

- ☐ **2 cups/250 g/8 oz flour**
- ☐ **1 tablespoon caster sugar**
- ☐ **155 g/5 oz butter, cut into small cubes**
- ☐ **1 egg yolk**
- ☐ **2-3 tablespoons iced water**
- ☐ **500 g/1 lb mixed berries**

MASCARPONE ORANGE FILLING
- ☐ **500 g/1 lb mascarpone**
- ☐ **³/₄ cup/185 mL/6 fl oz orange juice**
- ☐ **¹/₄ cup/60 mL/2 fl oz Cointreau (orange liqueur)**
- ☐ **1 teaspoon finely grated orange rind**
- ☐ **2 tablespoons icing sugar**

STRAWBERRY GLAZE
- ☐ **¹/₄ cup/75 g/2¹/₂ oz strawberry jam**
- ☐ **¹/₂ cup/125 mL/4 fl oz orange juice**
- ☐ **2 teaspoons gelatine**

1 Place flour, sugar and butter in a food processor and process until mixture resembles coarse bread crumbs. With machine running, add egg yolk and enough iced water to form a firm dough. Turn pastry onto a floured surface and knead lightly until smooth. Cover and refrigerate for 30 minutes.

2 Roll out pastry to fit a 23 cm/9 in square flan tin with a removable base. Line pastry case with nonstick baking paper, weigh down with uncooked rice and bake for 10-15 minutes. Remove rice and paper and cook for 5-10 minutes longer or until pastry is golden. Set aside to cool.

3 To make filling, place mascarpone, orange juice, Cointreau, orange rind and icing sugar in a bowl and beat until well combined.

4 Fill cold pastry case with filling and top with berries.

5 To make glaze, place jam and orange juice in a small saucepan, sprinkle over gelatine and heat over a low heat until gelatine dissolves. Remove from heat and set aside to cool slightly, then brush over tart.

Cook's tip: This tart can also be made in a 25 cm/10 in round flan tin. To make an alternative to mascarpone, place 250 g/8 oz softened cream cheese in a food processor and process until smooth. Add 250 mL/8 fl oz cream (double) and beat until mixture is creamy.

AUSTRIAN COFFEE CAKE

Serves 10
Oven temperature 180°C, 350°F, Gas 4

- ☐ **4 eggs, separated**
- ☐ **¹/₄ cup/60 g/2 oz caster sugar**
- ☐ **45 g/1¹/₂ oz ground almonds**
- ☐ **¹/₂ teaspoon vanilla essence**
- ☐ **3 teaspoons instant coffee powder dissolved in 4 teaspoons boiling water, cooled**
- ☐ **30 g/1 oz flour**

COFFEE CREAM
- ☐ **1 cup/250 mL/8 fl oz cream (double), whipped**
- ☐ **1 teaspoon instant coffee powder dissolved in 2 teaspoons boiling water, cooled**
- ☐ **1 tablespoon caster sugar**
- ☐ **2 tablespoons Tia Maria (coffee liqueur)**
- ☐ **chocolate-coated coffee beans or chocolate dots**
- ☐ **finely grated chocolate**

1 Place egg yolks and sugar in a mixing bowl and beat until thick and creamy. Beat in almonds, vanilla essence and coffee mixture.

2 Place egg whites in a bowl and beat until stiff peaks form. Sift flour over egg yolk mixture and fold in with egg white mixture. Spoon batter into a greased and lined 20 cm/8 in springform tin and bake for 20-25 minutes or until cooked when tested with a skewer. Allow to stand in tin for 10 minutes, before turning onto a wire rack to cool completely.

3 To make Coffee Cream, place ³/₄ cup/185 mL /6 fl oz cream in a bowl and beat in coffee mixture, sugar and Tia Maria. Cut cold cake in half horizontally and use a little of the coffee cream to sandwich halves together. Spread remaining Coffee Cream over top and sides of cake. Decorate top with coffee beans and grated chocolate. Chill and serve cut into slices.

CHOCOLATE CUPS WITH PEACH CREAM

Serves 6

☐ **440 g/14 oz milk chocolate, melted**

PEACH CREAM
☐ **310 mL/10 fl oz cream (double)**
☐ **2 tablespoons icing sugar, sifted**
☐ **2 peaches, peeled, stoned and flesh puréed**
☐ **¼ cup/60 mL/2 fl oz passion fruit pulp**

ALMOND PRALINE
☐ **1 cup/250 g/8 oz sugar**
☐ **1 cup/250 mL/8 fl oz water**
☐ **3 tablespoons slivered almonds, toasted**

PEACH COULIS
☐ **3 peaches, peeled, stoned and flesh puréed**
☐ **⅓ cup/90 mL/3 fl oz passion fruit pulp**

1   To make chocolate cups, cut six 15 cm/ 6 in squares of nonstick baking paper. Place small moulds or ramekins upside down on a tray and cover with paper squares. Spoon chocolate over base of mould and allow to run down sides of paper. Spread chocolate with a small spatula if it does not run freely. Set aside until chocolate sets, then carefully peel off paper.

2   To make Peach Cream, place cream in a bowl and whip until soft peaks form. Fold in icing sugar, peach purée and passion fruit pulp.

3   To make praline, place sugar and water in a saucepan and cook, stirring, over a low heat until sugar dissolves. Increase heat and simmer until syrup is golden. Place almonds on a greased baking tray and pour toffee over them. Set aside to harden then break into pieces and place in a food processor and process until toffee resembles coarse bread crumbs.

4   To make coulis, push peach purée and passion fruit pulp through a sieve to make a smooth purée. Add sugar to taste.

5   To assemble, flood serving plates with coulis, place chocolate cups on plates, fill with Peach Cream and sprinkle with praline.

Fresh Berry Tart, Chocolate Cups with Peach Cream

These rich little chocolate cakes filled with a raspberry cream and served with a bittersweet chocolate sauce are a perfect finale to any dinner party. Follow the step-by-step instructions and you will see just how easy this spectacular dessert is.

RASPBERRY CHOCOLATE TRUFFLE CAKES

Serves 8
Oven temperature 180°C, 350°F, Gas 4

- ☐ ½ cup/60 g/2 oz cocoa powder, sifted
- ☐ 1 cup/250 mL/8 fl oz boiling water
- ☐ 125 g/4 oz butter
- ☐ 1¾ cups/390 g/12½ oz caster sugar
- ☐ 1½ tablespoons raspberry jam
- ☐ 2 eggs
- ☐ 1²/₃ cups/200 g/6½ oz self-raising flour, sifted
- ☐ 410 g/13 oz dark chocolate, melted
- ☐ raspberries for garnishing

RASPBERRY CREAM
- ☐ 125 g/4 oz raspberries, puréed and sieved
- ☐ ½ cup/125 mL/4 fl oz cream (double), whipped

CHOCOLATE SAUCE
- ☐ 125 g/4 oz dark chocolate
- ☐ ½ cup/125 mL/4 fl oz water
- ☐ ¼ cup/60 g/2 oz caster sugar
- ☐ 1 teaspoon brandy (optional)

1   Combine cocoa powder and boiling water. Mix to dissolve and set aside to cool.

2   Place butter, sugar and jam in a bowl and beat until light and fluffy. Beat in eggs one at a time, adding a little flour with each egg. Fold remaining flour and cocoa mixture, alternately, into creamed mixture.

3   Spoon mixture into eight lightly greased ½ cup/125 mL/4 fl oz capacity ramekins or large muffin tins. Bake for 20-25 minutes or until cakes are cooked when tested with a skewer. Cool for 5 minutes then turn onto wire racks to cool. Turn cakes upside down and scoop out centre leaving a 1 cm/½ in shell. Spread each cake with chocolate to cover top and sides, then place right way up on a wire rack.

4   To make cream, fold raspberry purée into cream. Spoon cream into a piping bag fitted with a large nozzle. Carefully turn cakes upside down and pipe in cream to fill cavity. Place right way up on individual serving plates.

5   To make sauce, place chocolate and water in a small saucepan and cook over a low heat for 4-5 minutes or until chocolate melts. Add sugar and continue cooking, stirring constantly, until sugar dissolves. Bring just to the boil, then reduce heat and simmer, stirring, for 2 minutes. Set aside to cool for 5 minutes, then stir in brandy, if using. Cool sauce to room temperature.

To serve: Decorate plates with sauce.

1   Turn cakes upside down and scoop out centre of each cake leaving a 1 cm/½ in shell.

2   Carefully turn chocolate-coated cakes upside down and pipe in cream to fill cavity.

Plate Limoges

61

happy
EASTER

Easter is a special time for many people, not only because of its religious significance, but also because it's a time when families gather and special meals are prepared. Try this traditional Italian dessert, served at Easter, Christmas and weddings.

CASSATA ALLA SICILIANA

Serves 10
Oven temperature 180°C, 350°F, Gas 4

- [ ] **4 eggs**
- [ ] **¹/₂ cup/100 g/3¹/₂ oz caster sugar**
- [ ] **³/₄ cup/90 g/3 oz self-raising flour, sifted**
- [ ] **¹/₃ cup/90 mL/3 fl oz brandy**

CASSATA FILLING
- [ ] **¹/₂ cup/125 g/4 oz sugar**
- [ ] **4 teaspoons water**
- [ ] **375 g/12 oz ricotta cheese**
- [ ] **¹/₂ cup/125 mL/4 fl oz cream (double), whipped**
- [ ] **60 g/2 oz mixed peel, chopped**
- [ ] **100 g/3¹/₂ oz dark chocolate, finely chopped**
- [ ] **60 g/2 oz glacé cherries, quartered**
- [ ] **45 g/1¹/₂ oz unsalted pistachio nuts, chopped**

CHOCOLATE TOPPING
- [ ] **315 g/10 oz dark chocolate**
- [ ] **90 g/3 oz butter**

1   Place eggs in a large mixing bowl and beat until light and fluffy. Gradually add sugar, beating well after each addition until mixture is creamy. Fold in flour. Pour batter into a greased and lined 26 x 32 cm/10¹/₂ x 12³/₄ in Swiss roll tin and bake for 10-12 minutes or until cooked when tested with a skewer. Turn onto a wire rack to cool.

2   To make filling, place sugar and water in a saucepan and cook over a low heat, stirring constantly, until sugar dissolves. Remove from heat and set aside to cool. Place ricotta cheese in a food processor or blender and process until smooth. Transfer to a bowl and mix in syrup, cream, mixed peel, chocolate, cherries and nuts.

3   Line an 11 x 21 cm/4¹/₂ x 8¹/₂ in loaf dish with plastic food wrap. Cut cake into slices and sprinkle with brandy. Line base and sides of prepared dish with cake. Spoon filling into loaf dish and top with a final layer of cake. Cover and freeze until solid.

4   To make topping, place chocolate and butter in a saucepan and cook, stirring, over a low heat until melted and mixture is well blended. Allow to cool slightly.

5   Turn cassata onto a wire rack and cover with topping. Return to freezer until chocolate sets.

Serving suggestion: Decorate with glacé fruits and serve with whipped cream.

Cassata Alla Siciliana

Platter, cake server, cup and saucer Waterford Wedgwood *Material* In Material *Napkin* The Baytree Kitchen Shop

sweet
FINISHES

CHOCOLATE CHESTNUT TRUFFLES

Makes 36 truffles

- ☐ **100 g/3¹/₂ oz dark chocolate, melted**

CHESTNUT FILLING
- ☐ **¹/₄ cup/60 mL/2 fl oz cream (double)**
- ☐ **315 g/10 oz finely chopped dark chocolate**
- ☐ **30 g/1 oz butter**
- ☐ **2 tablespoons brandy**
- ☐ **¹/₂ cup/220 g/7 oz canned chestnut purée**

1   Spread the inside of 36 small aluminium foil cases with chocolate, set aside and allow to set.

2   To make filling, place cream in a small saucepan and bring to the boil. Remove pan from the heat, add chocolate and butter and whisk, using a balloon whisk, until chocolate is melted and mixture smooth. Whisk in brandy and stir in chestnut purée.

3   Transfer mixture to a bowl, cover with plastic food wrap and refrigerate for 2-3 hours.

4   Spoon mixture into a piping bag fitted with a small fluted nozzle and pipe swirls into chocolate cases. Chill for 1 hour or until firm. Store in the refrigerator in an airtight container for up to 2 weeks.

FLORENTINES

Makes 50
Oven temperature 180°C, 350°F, Gas 4

- ☐ **45 g/1¹/₂ oz butter**
- ☐ **2 tablespoons honey**
- ☐ **¹/₄ cup/45 g/1¹/₂ oz brown sugar**
- ☐ **¹/₄ cup/30 g/1 oz flour sifted with ¹/₄ teaspoon ground ginger**
- ☐ **45 g/1¹/₂ oz slivered almonds**
- ☐ **30 g/1 oz glacé cherries, chopped**
- ☐ **1 tablespoon mixed peel, finely chopped**

- ☐ **100 g/3¹/₂ oz dark chocolate, melted**

1   Place butter, honey and sugar in a saucepan and bring to the boil. Remove from heat and set aside to cool for 5 minutes.

2   Stir flour mixture, almonds and cherries into butter mixture. Drop teaspoons of mixture 8 cm/3 in apart onto baking trays lined with nonstick baking paper. Bake for 12-15 minutes or until brown and crisp. Allow florentines to stand on trays for 1 minute before carefully removing to wire racks to cool completely.

3   Spread underside of each florentine with melted chocolate. When nearly set, mark wavy lines in chocolate using a fork.

MINIATURE LIQUEUR PROFITEROLES

Makes 30
Oven temperature 250°C, 500°F, Gas 9

- ☐ **²/₃ cup/170 mL/5¹/₂ fl oz water**
- ☐ **45 g/1¹/₂ oz butter, cut into pieces**
- ☐ **¹/₂ cup/60 g/2 oz flour, sifted**
- ☐ **2 eggs**
- ☐ **icing sugar, sifted**
- ☐ **45 g/1¹/₂ oz dark chocolate, melted**

CREME PATISSIERE FILLING
- ☐ **2 cups/500 mL/16 fl oz milk**
- ☐ **5 egg yolks**
- ☐ **¹/₂ cup/100 g/3¹/₂ oz caster sugar**
- ☐ **2 tablespoons flour, sifted**
- ☐ **4 teaspoons cornflour, sifted**
- ☐ **1 teaspoon coffee dissolved in 1 teaspoon boiling water, cooled**
- ☐ **1 tablespoon Kahlua (coffee liqueur)**
- ☐ **¹/₂ teaspoon finely grated orange rind**
- ☐ **1 tablespoon Grand Marnier (orange liqueur)**

1   Place water and butter in a saucepan and slowly bring to the boil. As soon as the mixture boils, quickly stir in flour, using a wooden spoon. Cook over a low heat, beating constantly, for 2 minutes or until mixture is smooth and leaves sides of pan. Remove from heat and set aside to cool slightly. Beat in eggs, one at a time, beating well after each addition and until mixture is light and glossy.

2   Spoon batter into a piping bag fitted with a large fluted nozzle and pipe small swirls onto wetted baking trays lined with nonstick baking paper. Bake for 8 minutes, then prop oven door open using the handle of a wooden spoon and cook pastries for 10 minutes longer or until golden and crisp. Remove from oven, make a slit in the base of each profiterole, reduce oven temperature to 120°C/250°F/Gas ¹/₂ and cook profiteroles for 5 minutes longer or until centres dry out. Cool on wire racks.

3   To make filling, place milk in a saucepan and bring just to the boil, then remove from heat and set aside to cool for 10 minutes. Place egg yolks and sugar in a mixing bowl and beat until mixture is thick and creamy. Whisk in flour and cornflour, then slowly whisk in warm milk. Pour mixture into a clean saucepan and bring to the boil over a medium heat, beating constantly with a wooden spoon, until mixture thickens.

4   Divide mixture between two bowls and beat coffee mixture and Kahlua into one portion and orange rind and Grand Marnier into the other. Cover surface of both fillings with plastic food wrap and set aside to cool.

5   Spoon cold Kahlua filling into a piping bag fitted with a plain nozzle and pipe filling into half the profiteroles, through the slit in the base. Fill remaining profiteroles in the same way with Grand Marnier filling. Decorate profiteroles with melted chocolate.

SWEET CINNAMON BOWS

Makes 50
Oven temperature 190°C, 375°F, Gas 5

- ☐ **250 g/8 oz cream cheese**
- ☐ **250 g/8 oz unsalted butter**
- ☐ **1 cup/125 g/4 oz flour**
- ☐ **¼ cup/60 g/2 oz caster sugar**
- ☐ **2 teaspoons ground cinnamon**
- ☐ **icing sugar, sifted**

1   Roughly chop cream cheese and butter and set aside to stand at room temperature for 10 minutes. Place flour, sugar and cinnamon in a food processor and process briefly to sift. Add cream cheese and butter and process, using the pulse button, until mixture is combined. Take care not to overmix the dough. Turn dough onto a lightly floured surface, gather into a ball and knead briefly. Wrap dough in plastic food wrap and refrigerate for at least 1 hour.

2   Roll out dough to 3 mm/⅛ in thick. Cut dough into strips 1 cm wide and 20 cm/8 in long, using a pastry wheel or sharp knife. Shape each strip into a bow and place on baking trays lined with nonstick baking paper. Cover and refrigerate for 15 minutes. Bake for 5 minutes, then reduce temperature to 150°C/300°F/Gas 2 and cook for 10-15 minutes or until puffed and golden brown. Transfer to wire racks to cool. Store in airtight containers. Just prior to serving sprinkle with icing sugar.

HOT PUDDINGS
for cold nights

Y̶ou will find the puddings of childhood
memories in this chapter. Pancakes, crumbles and
self-saucing puddings along with soufflés and cobblers
will remind you of the puddings that mother used to
make. Served on their own or with custard and
ice cream these desserts are a wonderful
way to end a winter meal.

Top: Bow Napkin (see page 76)
Right: Rhubarb Soufflé
(recipe page 68)

Soufflé dish Mikasa Tableware Coffee service Villeroy & Boch Vase Waterford Wedgwood

RHUBARB SOUFFLE

Light, pretty and pink, this soufflé makes the best use of rhubarb that you will ever find.

Serves 8
Oven temperature 220°C, 425°F, Gas 7

- ☐ **500 g/1 lb rhubarb, trimmed and cut into 2.5 cm/1 in pieces**
- ☐ **¹/₂ cup/125 mL/4 fl oz water**
- ☐ **¹/₄ cup/60 g/2 oz sugar**
- ☐ **4 teaspoons cornflour blended with ¹/₄ cup/60 mL/2 fl oz water**
- ☐ **¹/₂ cup/100 g/3¹/₂ oz caster sugar**
- ☐ **5 egg whites**
- ☐ **icing sugar, sifted**

1　Place rhubarb, water and sugar in a saucepan and cook over a medium heat for 10 minutes or until rhubarb softens.

2　Stir in cornflour mixture and cook for 2-3 minutes longer or until mixture thickens. Add half the caster sugar and set aside to cool slightly.

3　Place egg whites in a large mixing bowl and beat until soft peaks form. Gradually add remaining sugar, beating well after each addition until mixture is thick and glossy. Fold in rhubarb mixture and spoon into a greased 20 cm/8 in soufflé dish. Bake for 15-20 minutes or until soufflé is well risen and golden brown. Dust with icing sugar and serve immediately.

BRANDIED PLUM CLAFOUTI

Serves 4
Oven temperature 180°C, 350°F, Gas 4

- ☐ **500 g/1 lb plums, quartered and stoned**
- ☐ **¹/₃ cup/90 mL/3 fl oz brandy**
- ☐ **2 tablespoons sugar**
- ☐ **¹/₄ cup/30 g/1 oz flour, sifted**
- ☐ **¹/₄ cup/60 g/2 oz caster sugar**
- ☐ **3 eggs, lightly beaten**
- ☐ **1 cup/250 mL/8 fl oz milk**

BRANDY ORANGE SAUCE
- ☐ **³/₄ cup/185 mL/6 fl oz orange juice**
- ☐ **2 tablespoons sugar**
- ☐ **¹/₂ teaspoon ground cinnamon**
- ☐ **2 teaspoons arrowroot blended with 4 teaspoons water**

1　Place plums and brandy in a bowl, sprinkle with sugar, cover and set aside to stand for 30 minutes. Drain plums and reserve liquid. Arrange plums in a lightly greased ovenproof dish.

2　Place flour and caster sugar in a bowl, add eggs and milk and stir until batter is smooth. Pour batter evenly over plums. Bake for 45-50 minutes or until firm.

3　To make sauce, place reserved brandy liquid, orange juice, sugar, cinnamon and arrowroot mixture in a small saucepan and cook over a medium heat, stirring constantly, until mixture boils and thickens. Accompany clafouti with Brandy Orange Sauce, and whipped cream if desired.

Cook's tip: Clafouti is a wonderful classic French pudding, traditionally made with fresh cherries. This recipe uses plums, but you might like to try apricots, peaches, nectarines or, of course, cherries.

TOFFEE FIGS WITH MARSALA SABAYON

Serves 4

- ☐ **1 cup/250 g/8 oz sugar**
- ☐ **¹/₂ cup/125 mL/4 fl oz water**
- ☐ **2 tablespoons brandy**
- ☐ **6 fresh figs, halved**

MARSALA SABAYON
- ☐ **4 egg yolks**
- ☐ **¹/₃ cup/90 g/3 oz sugar**
- ☐ **¹/₄ cup/60 mL/2 fl oz Marsala**

1　Place sugar and water in a saucepan and cook over a low heat, stirring constantly, until sugar dissolves. Stir in brandy, bring to the boil and cook until a golden colour. Remove from heat, dip figs in toffee, then plunge into iced water for a few seconds to harden toffee.

2　To make sabayon, place egg yolks and sugar in a large heatproof bowl over a saucepan of simmering water and cook, beating, for 5-10 minutes or until mixture forms a ribbon. Beat in Marsala. Spoon sabayon over figs and serve.

Cook's tip: This dessert is also delicious using other fresh fruit such as apples, pears, apricots and strawberries.

BLUEBERRY PANCAKES WITH BERRY SAUCE

Serves 4

- ☐ 1¹/₂ cups/185 g/6 oz self-raising flour
- ☐ ¹/₃ cup/90 g/3 oz caster sugar
- ☐ 2 teaspoons finely grated lemon rind
- ☐ 2 eggs, separated
- ☐ 1¹/₂ cups/375 mL/12 fl oz milk
- ☐ 30 g/1 oz butter, melted
- ☐ 155 g/5 oz blueberries

BERRY SAUCE
- ☐ ³/₄ cup/185 ml/6 fl oz water
- ☐ ¹/₄ cup/90 mL/3 fl oz light corn syrup
- ☐ 1 tablespoon lemon juice
- ☐ 4 teaspoons arrowroot blended with ¹/₃ cup/90 mL/3 fl oz water
- ☐ 90 g/3 oz raspberries
- ☐ 90 g/3 oz strawberries, hulled and quartered

1   Place flour, sugar and lemon rind in a bowl. Add egg yolks, milk and butter and mix until combined. Beat egg whites until soft peaks form, then fold into batter with blueberries. Cook spoonfuls of mixture in a lightly greased preheated frying pan for 2-3 minutes each side or until golden. Set aside to keep warm.

2   To make sauce, place water, corn syrup, lemon juice, arrowroot and raspberries in a saucepan and cook over a medium heat for 4-5 minutes or until sauce boils and thickens. Add strawberries to sauce and stir gently to combine. Spoon sauce over pancakes and serve immediately.

Plates Accoutrement Cook Shop Table Corso di Fiori

Brandied Plum Clafouti, Toffee Figs with Marsala Sabayon, Blueberry Pancakes with Berry Sauce

APPLE AND BERRY CRUMBLE

Blueberries have been used to make this delicious crumble, but you might like to try blackberries, raspberries or strawberries instead.

Serves 6
Oven temperature 180°C, 350°F, Gas 4

- ☐ ¼ cup/60 g/2 oz caster sugar
- ☐ ½ cup/125 mL/4 fl oz water
- ☐ 4 green apples, peeled, cored and sliced
- ☐ 440 g/14 oz canned blueberries, drained

CRUMBLE TOPPING
- ☐ 1¾ cups/250 g/8 oz crushed shortbread biscuits
- ☐ 45 g/1½ oz unsalted butter, softened
- ☐ 4 tablespoons ground almonds
- ☐ 2 tablespoons demerara sugar
- ☐ ½ teaspoon ground cinnamon
- ☐ 1 egg yolk
- ☐ 1½ tablespoons cream (double)

1 Place sugar and water in a saucepan and cook over a medium heat, stirring constantly, until sugar dissolves. Bring to the boil, then add apples and cook, over a low heat, for 8-10 minutes or until apples are tender. Remove from heat and set aside to cool.

2 Drain apples and combine with blueberries. Spoon apple mixture into a greased, shallow ovenproof dish.

3 To make topping, place crushed biscuits, butter, almonds, sugar, cinnamon, egg yolk and cream in a mixing bowl and mix until just combined. Sprinkle topping over apple mixture and bake for 20-25 minutes or until golden.

Serving suggestion: This crumble is delicious served with natural yogurt or fruit-flavoured yogurt.

PEACH AND BLACKBERRY COBBLER

Serves 6
Oven temperature 180°C, 350°F, Gas 4

- ☐ 2 x 440 g/14 oz canned sliced peaches, drained
- ☐ 440 g/14 oz canned blackberries, drained
- ☐ 4 teaspoons cornflour blended with ¼ cup/60 mL/2 fl oz water
- ☐ 1 tablespoon brown sugar

COBBLER DOUGH
- ☐ ¼ cup/30 g/1 oz flour
- ☐ ½ cup/60 g/2 oz self-raising flour
- ☐ 2 tablespoons caster sugar
- ☐ 60 g/2 oz butter
- ☐ 1 egg, lightly beaten
- ☐ 2 teaspoons milk

1 To make dough, sift together flour and self-raising flour into a mixing bowl. Stir in caster sugar. Rub in butter, using fingertips, until mixture resembles fine bread crumbs. Make a well in the centre of the flour mixture and mix in egg and milk to form a soft dough.

2 Arrange peaches and blackberries in a greased, shallow ovenproof dish and pour over cornflour mixture. Drop heaped spoonfuls of batter around edge of fruit mixture and sprinkle with brown sugar. Bake for 30-35 minutes or until cobbler topping is golden.

Serving suggestion: Delicious served with fresh berries and whipped cream.

Quick ideas from a CAN OF FRUIT

Canned fruit is the perfect quick dessert, whether you serve it on its own, with ice cream or cream, or use it as a base for a crumble. The following quick ideas for dressing up a can of fruit will serve four.

Easy Fruit Fool: Any canned fruit can be used to make this fool. Apricots, peaches and plums are always popular choices. To make the fool, drain a 440 g/14 oz can of fruit. Place the fruit in a food processor or blender and process until smooth. Whip ½ cup/125 mL/4 fl oz cream (double) with 1-2 tablespoons sugar, according to taste. Fold fruit purée into cream. Spoon into individual serving glasses and chill until required.

Peaches in Cinnamon Syrup: Canned peaches take on a whole new taste when prepared in this way. Place 4 tablespoons orange juice, 2 tablespoons caster sugar, 1 tablespoon lemon juice, 1 tablespoon Cointreau (orange liqueur), 3 tablespoons water, 6 whole cloves and 1 cinnamon stick in a small saucepan and bring to the boil. Reduce heat and simmer for 5 minutes or until mixture is syrupy. Drain 8 canned peach halves, add to syrup and toss to coat. Place 2 peach halves on each of four serving plates and spoon over remaining syrup.

Lychees in Cointreau: Drain a 440 g/14 oz can of lychees and divide between four individual serving bowls. Peel and chop 1 orange and add to bowls with lychees, toss to combine. Sprinkle fruit with a little Cointreau and chill until required.

Apple and Berry Crumble,
Peach and Blackberry Cobbler

HAZELNUT CREPES WITH ORANGES

For the topping on these delicious crêpes you may prefer to use lemon in place of the lime.

Serves 4

- ☐ ³/₄ cup/90 g/3 oz flour
- ☐ 90 g/3 oz hazelnuts, ground
- ☐ 1 egg, lightly beaten
- ☐ 2 teaspoons hazelnut or vegetable oil
- ☐ 1¹/₄ cups/315 mL/10 fl oz milk

ORANGE AND LIME TOPPING
- ☐ 1 lime
- ☐ ¹/₂ cup/100 g/3¹/₂ oz caster sugar
- ☐ ¹/₄ cup/60 mL/2 fl oz ginger wine
- ☐ 2 oranges, peeled, white pith removed and segmented

1   Sift flour into a large mixing bowl, then stir in hazelnuts. Make a well in the centre of the flour mixture and stir in egg, oil and milk. Mix to a smooth batter, cover and set aside to stand for 30 minutes.

2   To make topping, remove rind from lime using a vegetable peeler and cut into thin strips. Set aside. Squeeze juice from lime and place in a saucepan with sugar and ginger wine. Cook over a medium heat, stirring constantly, until sugar dissolves. Bring to the boil, then reduce heat and simmer for 4 minutes. Remove pan from heat and stir in lime rind and orange segments. Set aside to cool slightly.

3   Pour 2-3 tablespoons batter into a heated, greased crêpe pan and cook over a medium heat until lightly browned on both sides. Remove from pan and repeat with remaining mixture to make eight crêpes.

4   To serve, fold crêpes into triangles, place two on each serving plate, spoon topping over and serve immediately.

NUTTY PLUM CRUMBLE

Serves 6
Oven temperature 180°C, 350°F, Gas 4

- ☐ **4 x 440 g/14 oz canned dark plums, drained and ³/₄ cup/ 185 mL/6 fl oz liquid reserved**
- ☐ **1 teaspoon finely grated orange rind**

CRUMBLE TOPPING
- ☐ **¹/₂ cup/60 g/2 oz flour**
- ☐ **1 teaspoon ground mixed spice**
- ☐ **60 g/2 oz butter, chopped**
- ☐ **¹/₃ cup/60 g/2 oz brown sugar**
- ☐ **90 g/3 oz hazelnuts, chopped**

1   To make topping, place flour and spice in a mixing bowl. Rub in butter, using fingertips, until mixture resembles fine bread crumbs. Stir in sugar and hazelnuts.

2   Combine plums and orange rind. Spoon plums and liquid into a greased, shallow ovenproof dish. Sprinkle topping over and bake for 30-35 minutes or until topping is golden.

Serving suggestion: Accompany with whipped cream or yogurt for a really wonderful family dessert.

Light blue plate Limoges Oval crumble dish Mikasa Tableware

*Hazelnut Crêpes with Oranges,
Nutty Plum Crumble*

welcome
THANKSGIVING

Thanksgiving is a special time in the United States when the safe landing of the Pilgrim Fathers in the New World over 350 years ago is celebrated. Pumpkin pie is one of the culinary delights served at the traditional Thanksgiving meal.

SPICY PUMPKIN PIE

Serves 8
Oven temperature 200°C, 400°F, Gas 6

PASTRY
- ☐ **1 cup/125 g/4 oz flour**
- ☐ **¹/₂ teaspoon baking powder**
- ☐ **100 g/3¹/₂ oz butter, cut into pieces**
- ☐ **1¹/₂ tablespoons caster sugar**
- ☐ **1 egg yolk**
- ☐ **¹/₂-1 tablespoon water**

SPICY PUMPKIN FILLING
- ☐ **280 g/8 oz pumpkin, cooked and puréed**
- ☐ **2 eggs, lightly beaten**
- ☐ **¹/₂ cup/125 g/4 oz sour cream**
- ☐ **¹/₂ cup/125 mL/4 fl oz cream (double)**
- ☐ **¹/₄ cup/90 g/ 3 oz golden syrup**
- ☐ **¹/₂ teaspoon ground nutmeg**
- ☐ **¹/₂ teaspoon ground mixed spice**
- ☐ **¹/₂ teaspoon ground cinnamon**

1   To make pastry, sift flour and baking powder into a mixing bowl. Rub in butter, with fingertips, until mixture resembles coarse bread crumbs, then stir in sugar. Make a well in the centre and mix in egg yolk and enough water to mix to a firm dough. Turn onto a floured surface and knead lightly until smooth. Wrap in plastic food wrap and refrigerate for 30 minutes.

2   To make filling, place pumpkin, eggs, sour cream, cream, golden syrup, nutmeg, mixed spice and cinnamon in a mixing bowl and beat until smooth and well combined.

3   Roll pastry out and line a greased 23 cm/9 in flan tin with removable base. Spoon filling into pastry case. Bake for 20 minutes then reduce heat to 160°C/325°F/Gas 3 and bake for 25-30 minutes longer or until filling is set and pastry golden. Allow to stand in tin for 5 minutes before removing. Serve hot, warm or cold with whipped cream.

Spicy Pumpkin Pie

elegant NAPKINS

An elegantly folded napkin adds a special touch to any place setting. Follow these step-by-step instructions to see just how easy it is to fold wonderful-looking napkins and use the ideas throughout this book to add that final touch.

BOW NAPKIN

This is a pretty way to fold a napkin that has a lace corner or edge. You will also require 90 cm/1 yd of wide ribbon for each napkin .

1   Starch and iron the napkin well and fold into quarters. With one of the points of the napkin facing you, fold under the two outer corners and iron the napkin flat.

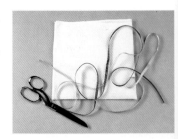

2   Fold the ends of the ribbon in half horizontally and cut diagonally, to give decorative points.

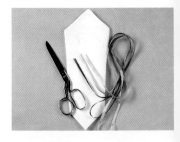

3   Lay the ribbon flat, wrong side up, and place the napkin on top of it and tie bow as shown.

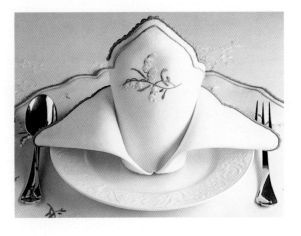

SIMPLE ELEGANCE

1 Fold the napkin in half diagonally to form a triangle, then fold each corner up to the apex to form a square.

2 Turn the napkin over so that the loose flaps are sitting on your work surface and fold the lower corner up slightly.

3 Fold under the outer corners on a slight diagonal and lightly press folds in place.

THE BISHOP'S HAT

This napkin fold looks great sitting on a flat surface, on a plate or in a glass when the flaps drape attractively over the sides of the plate or glass.

1 Fold the napkin in half diagonally to form a triangle, then fold each corner up to the apex to form a square.

2 Turn the napkin around, so that the free ends face you, then turn the free ends back on themselves and fold under the remaining triangle.

3 Turn the napkin over, so that the two small triangles are on your work surface, then bring the two outer corners together and tuck one flap into the folds of the other. Place the napkin with the front of the hat facing you and pull the loose flaps down as shown.

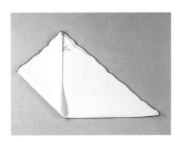

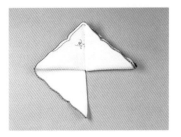

INDEX